"If you're a mama who has asked all th about . . . ?' questions regarding the well-being of your children or your competency as a mom, you're in good company. Courtney offers a hand to hold through her relatable and vulnerable tale of her own anxiety related to motherhood. For my patients who have struggled with worry, fear, or anxiety, they most want to know that they aren't crazy and they aren't alone. *Mama's Got Anxiety* assures the reader they aren't alone and their anxiety around child-rearing doesn't detract from their worth or effectiveness as a mother."

> **Dr. Michelle Bengtson**, award-winning author
> of *Breaking Anxiety's Grip* and host of the
> podcast *Your Hope-Filled Perspective*

"Courtney Devich's new book *Mama's Got Anxiety* came to me at a perfect time. After sharing about my own struggles with fear in *Mothering by the Book*, I was well aware of how fear and anxiety steal joy from our families and that I had steps to overcome. But new fears had come up for me in the midst of a new season. Courtney's book had helpful reminders for recapturing peace as well as scriptural reminders that God has us and He will never forsake us. Courtney reminds us of His trustworthiness and gives the fearful mama hopeful insights for creating calm."

> **Jennifer Pepito**, author of *Mothering by the Book*

"This book is so needed for mamas in our world right now! Courtney reminds us of an important truth: anxiety's voice and God's voice are not the same. She guides readers into God's presence using relatable stories. She encourages us to drop shame and pick up His mercy and grace as practical strategies are implemented into a new way of thinking and living. As a survivor and overcomer of anxiety, I am so grateful we have this tool!"

> **Caris Snider**, bestselling author, speaker, podcaster,
> and certified professional life coach

"If you are looking for a friend who has traveled through the trenches of anxiety and is eager to remind you that you are not alone and there is hope—Courtney Devich is that friend. Any woman who suffers from anxiety rooted in or exacerbated by motherhood will find great comfort, biblical encouragement, and practical tools in the pages of *Mama's Got Anxiety*."

Becky Keife, author of *The Simple Difference* and *No Better Mom for the Job*

"As a fellow mama who has struggled with anxiety (and has experienced how it can amplify in motherhood), I found myself nodding along with Courtney's book and thinking, 'This is exactly how I've felt.' For any mom struggling with anxiety and feeling like your faith must not be strong enough, this book will be a calming reassurance that God is right there with you in anxiety and He is not done with you."

Kelli Bachara, mental health therapist and writer

Mama's got Anxiety

But It's Not Going to Steal Her Joy

Courtney Devich

Revell

a division of Baker Publishing Group
Grand Rapids, Michigan

© 2023 by Courtney M. Devich

Published by Revell
a division of Baker Publishing Group
Grand Rapids, Michigan
www.revellbooks.com

Printed in the United States of America

Library of Congress Cataloging-in-Publication Data
Names: Devich, Courtney M., 1990– author.
Title: Mama's got anxiety : but it's not going to steal her joy / Courtney Devich.
Description: Grand Rapids, Michigan : Revell, a division of Baker Publishing Group, [2023] | Includes bibliographical references.
Identifiers: LCCN 2022052022 | ISBN 9780800742799 (paperback) | ISBN 9780800745042 (casebound) | ISBN 9781493443468 (ebook)
Subjects: LCSH: Mothers—Religious life. | Anxiety—Religious Aspects—Christianity. | Motherhood—Religious aspects—Christianity.
Classification: LCC BV4529.18 .D48 2023 | DDC 248.8/431—dc23/eng/20230217
LC record available at https://lccn.loc.gov/2022052022

The author is represented by the literary agency of William K. Jensen Literary Agency.

23   24   25   26   27   28   29   7   6   5   4   3   2   1

To William and Adelyn,
my biggest worries in life
and my greatest joys

Contents

Introduction

Let's Take Back Our Joy

You're anxious. You wouldn't have picked up this book if you weren't.

You may even have anxiety about having anxiety. (Yes, that's a thing.)

It's not just the common, everyday worries or the occasional tossing and turning at night—no, you're experiencing some real, debilitating anxiety.

I know; I've been there.

I've been there and back . . . and found my way there again.

And now, I'm currently coming from there.

I had coped with my anxiety for many years and had even been off my medication since the birth of my first child. I handled the pressures of work and everyday life without any real issues. But with anxiety, we all have triggers, and mine is the fear of something bad happening to my kids. So when a global pandemic hit in 2020, my anxiety peaked. I felt like I had absolutely no control over my life and what was going on around me. While the world turned upside down and the store shelves were wiped of toilet paper, I was consumed with fear of this virus taking my babies from me. There was a threat outside my house, and I didn't know how my kids would react if they got it. On top of it all, it was a threat I could not physically see.

After a year of complete isolation, I couldn't do it anymore. My anxiety would rise any time my children touched something from the store or came in contact with the outside world. I would spray and wipe everything down. If there was a way to have something delivered to my house, I found it, and I lived within the four walls of my home for a whole year. (For me, that's a long time to go without a Target run. Thank You, Lord, for online shopping.) I cut my family off from the rest of the world, and I could feel my anxiety getting worse with every passing day.

I also quit my job due to the pandemic. Having just become a stay-at-home mom, I felt I wasn't able to enjoy this season of life at home with my littles. All of the things I should have been able to do with my kids—playdates with neighbors, going to the zoo or the park, taking them swimming—I was unable to do. Instead of sitting back and soaking in this time I had at home with my kids, I was hiding in my house, living one long anxiety attack after the other.

My anxiety was taking the joy out of motherhood.

It was in the middle of a panic attack during the wee hours of the morning when I first felt God nudge me to write this book. I could not sleep, and my mind was racing, but I didn't know what I was worried about. My heart was racing so fast I was having a hard time breathing while lying in bed, so I got up and went to the living room. Sitting on the couch with my head in my hands and my knees pressed up against my chest, I tried to take each breath in slowly. I could feel it coming on, the panic attack. Again, about what, I couldn't tell you.

I started crying and asking God to take it all away. I prayed He would take my pain away and give me some peace for my anxiety. It was the same prayer I had prayed for months. I began to calm down, but I couldn't go back to sleep; my mind began to wander, and I started thinking about you. Yes, I'm talking about *you*, Mama.

I began to think about all the moms who suffer from anxiety. I knew there were moms who were too embarrassed or proud to get help. They probably were beating themselves up, thinking anxiety was a sign God had abandoned them. They may think it was a spiritual issue and not even know anxiety is a medical condition. I knew there were moms who, after sharing their struggles with others, were told to "just pray some more" and left feeling worse about themselves. Well, after thinking all of that, I knew I had to do something.

I knew I had to write this book.

I thought about how I wanted to approach this—how to approach you—and what words I needed to say. I've read a lot about being a Christian with anxiety, and let me tell you, not all books made me feel better. Some books gave me comfort and hope, but very few. Others left me feeling ashamed of my condition or how I felt (which is not the result you want from a self-help book). They addressed it from the standpoint that having anxiety is unbelief, and we're sinners for not trusting God more.

I'm not going to do that.

I'm not going to refer to anxiety as sin. I'm not here to condemn you. You live with anxiety, so you know it's real; and for some of us, it's an imbalance of the chemicals in our brains. I will not make you feel ashamed for having anxiety.

I'm not going to call it unbelief. You know your relationship with God better than anyone. I'm not going to assume that because you get anxious, you don't believe enough. I'll point you to Scripture and talk about how you can better your relationships with God so you may cope better. But I'm not going to tell you that you're praying wrong or not believing hard enough, because that's not helpful when people say those things to you. You're a mom fighting through anxiety, and you need the comfort that another mom is there with you (Hey, I'm right here!) and the hope from God that can and *will* get us through this.

I want to approach this as two friends who share the same struggle. So imagine we're sitting at a Starbucks, drinking coffee (I love coffee, first thing you should know about me) and talking about anxiety and our faith. Imagine I'm a good friend—no judgment. (And seriously, no judgment. I get super vulnerable in these pages and share some pretty weird, downright embarrassing stuff.) We're just two mamas who feel like their anxiety has gotten out of control since becoming mothers, and it's robbing us of our joy in motherhood.

Now, I'm going to be honest here—I don't know if I'll ever be healed of my anxiety. I know, how can I say that if I'm here writing a book about Jesus and anxiety? Yes, I do believe Jesus heals. I've seen His work in the lives of others and in my own life. Jesus heals; I'm not denying that. And He may very well heal me someday. But what I'm saying is, I may have seasons when my anxiety is heightened and it's overwhelming (like the season I'm currently coming out of), and I may have seasons when it doesn't bother me as much. It may come and go, off and on, for the rest of my life.

But . . .

What I *know* is when I get to the gates of heaven and see God's face for the first time, I want Him to say this: "You've suffered a lot, My daughter, but you never took your eyes off of Me." Even if I have this mental illness for the rest of my life, I'm staying focused on Him, because He's my source of strength. And that, my friend, is where we'll find joy in our anxiety.

Before we get started, though, I feel like I have to tell you something: I'm not a doctor. I have no medical or counseling background. I'm also not a pastor, nor do I have advanced knowledge of theology. I am a stay-at-home mom who is a former human resource professional. My degree is in business, not in psychology. And most days, I am in my pajamas running after kids and wiping snotty noses. I'm a mom—just like you—who has lived with anxiety my entire life and relies on my faith to get by. So before we dig into this, I want to make it clear my book is not meant to substitute for the use of a professional. In fact, if you haven't already, I urge you to seek the help of a professional. (Don't worry; we'll talk more about this later.) Now, here's what you can expect from this book.

Throughout the chapters of this book, I've identified common feelings, symptoms, and thoughts we believe as Christian moms who suffer from anxiety. Some of these are straight-up symptoms and some are thoughts we have about ourselves as we battle anxiety every day. And some are perceptions (or even lies) we've told ourselves for years that the enemy wants us to believe. It is my goal to provide you with the strength and truth behind these feelings by pointing you to what God has to say.

At the end of each chapter, you'll find a "Baby Steps" section. Everyone always kept telling me to just take baby steps as I was trying to overcome my debilitating anxiety and take my life back. When your mind has been set to "anxious" for quite a while, it's all about focusing on the baby steps and tackling them all one by one. Of course, you may find yourself reverting every now and again, and that's okay. That's normal. That's your anxiety saying, "I want to be in the driver's seat now." But these steps I'm giving you consist of action items and some reflection questions to help you in your journey toward joy. I want you to focus on taking this all one step at a time. We're going to find a way forward together, I promise.

It's my hope that by the time you finish this book, you'll no longer feel ashamed of your anxiety, and you'll be able to cope with the everyday things that make you anxious.

It's my goal to help you take back the wheel from your anxiety and take back your joy in motherhood.

Let's get started.

Dear God,

I pray for the mama whose hands have found this book. Father, I pray she finds hope from Your Word. I pray she seeks You and Your strength. I pray You give her peace by silencing the anxious thoughts in her head. But more than anything, I pray that, by the end of this book, she knows her anxiety has a purpose, her anxiety is not a sign of weak faith, and her

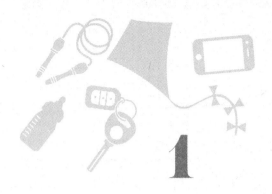

I'm a Mom—It's My Job to Worry

(Feeling: Motherhood has made my anxiety worse)

God knew I would have anxiety.

He knew I'd be a worrier, and He knew it would be a big hurdle in my life—I believe that. He also knew this hurdle would draw me closer to Him at a time in my life when the world seemed to be crumbling and my fear was consuming. And He knew the one thing that could trigger my anxiety even more—the one thing in this world that would cripple me: losing my kids.

Oh, the joys of motherhood. We never really have a care in the world until we become a mom, and then those little beings become the most important things in our lives. But I'm getting a little ahead of myself here. Let's back up and I'll give you a little bit of my story.

I've suffered from anxiety since I was a kid. I always obsessed and worried over the future. As a ten-year-old, I worried about what my major would be in college. I job shadowed at a veterinarian clinic at the age of twelve, convinced I had to have my college plans solidified before middle school. I could never sleep through the night before the first day of school because I worried about whether I'd have any friends in my class or if I'd like my teacher. I was even afraid of sleeping by myself in my own bed. I was constantly going to my (younger) sister's room and sleeping in her bed; and I'm not talking about as a five-year-old—we're talking much older than that. As a teenager, I fixated on career choices, marriage, and children, always looking to the future and being filled with worry about it.

Then, when I was nineteen years old, I let myself get so anxious about my job that I began having chest pains and sought the help of a cardiologist. They put me through all sorts of tests and did not find anything wrong with my heart, but I ended up being diagnosed with anxiety and was put on medication. I did well with medication and was able to handle life more easily. I was still awake at night with worry, but my worries were more understandable and less irrational. Otherwise, I was coping fine and could face work without my cheeks getting red as my heart started racing about the stress of my job.

And then motherhood happened.

Both of my children showed up early. William was born at thirty-six weeks, and I was induced with Adelyn at thirty-seven weeks. This made me anxious right from the start of motherhood. Every doctor's appointment, I panicked about whether they had gained a sufficient amount of weight. Every week they were unable to breastfeed, I beat myself up for my body's inability to do what it was created to do. Every night, I sat there and watched them sleep. Some nights I'd hold them all night long in my arms, rocking in the chair so I could hear those little breaths. Other nights I would put them straight in bed with me, so I knew they were breathing. (I know this probably wasn't the safest, but it helped with my anxiety!)

I imagined the worst happening. I read about SIDS and made sure the swaddle was wrapped tight enough. I fixated on other things that could go wrong with my babies: the possibility of them drowning in the tub, the possibility of them choking on their food, the possibility of them rolling over on their belly in their bassinet and suffocating in the middle of the night. I was like a doomsday Debbie Downer who forgot to sit back, relax, and enjoy the early days of motherhood. I was exhausted with the normal sleep deprivation that comes with a newborn, but even more because I would lie awake all night in a state of panic.

It's a given; we all worry about how we're doing as a mother, especially when we're new moms and feel unequipped for this. (If that's you, you're doing a great job, and you've got this!) There are typical, normal motherhood concerns, and then there's crippling anxiety where you're locking yourself in the bathroom because you don't want your kids to see you have a panic attack. This is when we need God the most, so let's take a look at Scripture.

The Psalms are comforting, and they cover such a wide variety of emotions we face as humans. But I think what I love most about the psalmist's words is how many of them address depression and anxiety. In Psalm 94:18–19, the psalmist writes,

> When I said, "My foot is slipping,"
>   your unfailing love, LORD, supported me.
> *When anxiety was great within me,*
>   *your consolation brought me joy.*
>   (Emphasis added so you can highlight that baby
>   and see where I'm going with this.)

Some translations, like the Christian Standard Bible and the New Living Translation, use the word *comfort* instead of *consolation* in this verse, but the word *consolation* means to provide comfort.

I like this excerpt because it's not the typical "hand your anxieties over to God, and He'll take care of it all for you" approach. No. He didn't say you're not going to have anxious thoughts in life, but these verses promise He's going to comfort you when you do. He's going to support you and take care of you if you feel like you're slipping into the depths of your anxiety or going through a season where your anxiety is high. He's the strength you need to face your anxiety head-on.

His comfort will bring your joy back in motherhood.

If you feel like your anxiety is worse since becoming a mother, it probably is. If you've developed anxiety after becoming a mom, well, welcome to the club. To quote my own mother, "I'm a mom; it's my job to worry." It's in our DNA to love our kids unconditionally and fiercely. However, there comes a point where those worries become debilitating, when you suffer from an anxiety disorder and the fear takes over so much to the point where you barely enjoy motherhood (let alone life in general) because of it.

Someday, those beautiful babies will leave our homes (or maybe they already have for you) and time is too precious with them. We don't want to be consumed with our anxiety and miss out on all the joys of motherhood, because we know how darn fast those kids grow up.

Let's not let anxiety win.

Let's take our joy back.

Adrenaline Mode

Boom!

"What was that?" I nudged my husband, Billy. His eyes were open, he had heard the noise too. At least I wasn't imagining things.

"I'm not sure," he said. "Let me go check."

I had just put Adelyn back in her crib after her 4:00 a.m. feeding. At first, I thought maybe William had fallen out of his bed, but that was not the case.

"The house two doors down is on fire!" Billy rushed into the room, panicking. "I'm going out there to see if everyone got out!"

I didn't think I heard him right at first. I thought, *This is a dream, right? This isn't real.* I got out of bed and looked out the window. The sound we'd heard was the neighbor's car catching fire. The whole garage and roof of their house were ablaze.

My mind and heart started racing. A house fire had been a fear of mine since becoming a mother, and now I was witnessing it first-hand. We rushed outside and made sure everyone had gotten out of the house safely. Everyone made it out except the dog (spoiler alert: the fireman later saved the dog). I immediately called 911. My brain was so foggy that I was unable to tell them the address of the house; I was unable to think or even speak clearly. My mind then moved to the house next to us, the one between the house on fire and our house. They're an older couple and I didn't think they would hear what was going on and wake up in time. But the neighbors were already on it, banging on the elderly couple's door. Just as the couple evacuated their home, the fire jumped to the top of their house's roof. The fire didn't waste any time and spread quickly. The whole side of the second house was immediately engulfed in flames.

Everyone got out safely, the fire department was still on their way, but Billy and I began to panic—our house was the next one in the line of fire.

We rushed inside and woke William. We gathered clothes, then I ran for the baby bottles and the formula. My hands were shaking as I tried to scoop formula into my travel container. And, yeah, I have no idea why I didn't think to just take the whole container; those thoughts were not at the top of my mind. Nothing was at the top of my mind. My chest felt like it was going to explode. *I am having a panic attack*, I thought. *What do I take? What if we are going to lose everything in our house and I have only a few minutes to get what I want—what is it?* Of course, Billy knew what to get. He grabbed baby books, photo albums, social security cards, clothes, blankets, and all the baby essentials. And there I was, still struggling to scoop up some darn formula, spilling it all over the countertop as my hands were shaking uncontrollably.

It was total adrenaline mode. It was fight-or-flight, the threat detection hormone kicking in. We hear about these moments. Moments where we can be in complete distress, but we're magically able to react and our instincts kick in. And our instincts acted exactly as they should have that night. All of our neighbors reacted quickly and got out of their houses safely. The neighbors from the first house lost all of their belongings, but God was there through it all; He made sure everyone woke up and got out in time.

What happens when you're in constant adrenaline mode? When you're in constant fear and that fight-or-flight response is kicked up to high gear and you don't know how to turn it down?

That's what living with anxiety is like.

Gosh, do I know what that's like. And if you can relate to that feeling at all, or if you experience this every day, I'm sure glad you've stumbled across my book! You may have been told to just quit worrying so much and made to feel like it's all your fault, but there is a medical side to anxiety.

Perhaps you are a mom who has had anxiety for many years, and you've done counseling, sought biblical counsel with your pastor, and taken all the medications and supplements you can find. But for a moment, let's pretend you are new to this. Maybe you've recently been diagnosed with anxiety, or perhaps you've started feeling some symptoms, done a few Google searches, and now you're reading this book to learn a little more about what to do. To help you take your joy back, we need to take a look at some of the basics—specifically, what anxiety disorders are. (Yes, this could get boring, and maybe you already know all of this, but please follow along with me. I've got an important point I'm going to make!)

We hear the word *anxiety* thrown around a lot these days, and it's because anxiety disorders are the most common mental illness in the United States, affecting nearly one in five adults.[1] Although anxiety is pretty popular (not that this is a popularity contest), women are more than twice as likely as men to be diagnosed with anxiety at any time in their lives.[2] Read that again and take that in. *Women are more than twice as likely.* Why is that? Well, I have a hunch but, again, I'm not the doctor. However, here's one of the reasons I think contributes.

Studies show during pregnancy, and even during the postpartum period, a woman's brain goes through a slew of changes (structurally and hormonally). These changes help her react to her baby's needs and give her maternal behaviors. However, these brain changes also put her at a higher risk for developing a mental illness—not just during pregnancy or postpartum, but potentially relapsing from a preexisting anxiety disorder.[3] (See, I told you motherhood contributes to anxiety!)

Now, maybe you're not a birth mom. Maybe your motherhood journey includes adoption or foster care. You may be thinking, *I didn't have all of those pregnancy hormonal changes, so where did my anxiety come from?* Maybe you haven't had anxiety your whole life (like I have) but developed it postadoption or after you became a foster mom. Just as you developed that "mom gene" and those mom instincts kicked in with your child, you can still go on to develop anxiety. There are a whole bunch of circumstantial and stressful events that can contribute to your anxiety. Anxiety about whether the birth mom will change her mind and if the adoption will fall through. Anxiety about bonding issues. Anxiety about lack of control through the birth process and decisions made by the birth mom. Anxiety about all the emotions you're feeling, maybe even grief because of a history of child loss and infertility. Anxiety about having a relationship with the birth family if you did an open adoption. Anxiety about bonding with your foster child if you're a foster mom. Anxiety about whether your other kids will get along with your foster child. Anxiety about reunification and having to say goodbye to your foster child. Anxiety about your foster child's well-being once they reunite with their birth mother and/or father.

We are all just a bunch of anxious moms.

No matter your motherhood journey, anxiety is very common among mothers. There may not be as much research about post-adoption or foster care motherhood anxiety, but if that's your story, you know it's all too real. No matter your life story or at what point you developed anxiety, it's important you understand what goes on in that brain of yours when anxiety takes over.

First of all, we're not talking about a one-size-fits-all type of anxiety disorder. There are several types of disorders and many other factors (or events) that contribute to anxiety—social anxiety disorder, panic disorder, and phobia-related disorders are a few.[4] (And of course, you can have several of these, not just one or the other. Yeah . . . I know.) For the purpose of this book, we'll focus on generalized anxiety disorder (GAD)—the most common anxiety disorder that can affect our lives in a million different ways.

The National Institute of Mental Health describes it this way: "GAD usually involves a persistent feeling of anxiety or dread that interferes with how you live your life. It is not the same as occasionally worrying about things or experiencing anxiety due to stressful life events."[5]

I'll give you my description of it: we worry, and we're scared a lot. Plain and simple, am I right?

We worry about everything and obsess about stuff that might be nothing to other people. We let our minds wander, imagining a ton of worst-case scenarios. We can spend hours thinking while our brains jump from one thought to the next. We can get anxious about something to the point where our hearts race and we feel dizzy, shaky, or light-headed. We get nervous about things. We have a feeling of impending doom. We get irritable. And we have difficulty concentrating and sleeping.

So what exactly causes anxiety? For some, it can be genetic or biological factors that come into play as part of their brain's makeup. Our brains have chemicals called neurotransmitters that send messages throughout our body about how we are feeling. When these chemicals are imbalanced, or these hormones are being released too often, this can cause anxiety. And sometimes it's a traumatic experience that triggers it. Any emotional or psychological trauma or ongoing string of stressful events can also lead to an anxiety disorder.

Since this is a book for moms, let's take a moment to look at postpartum anxiety. Every mama worries when they first bring their baby home, thinking *I have no clue what I am doing!* We worry about things such as whether our babies are getting enough milk from nursing or if they're warm enough in their swaddle. But postpartum anxiety is taking that to the next level. It's not postpartum depression or "baby blues" (although, a mom can have both at the same time). With postpartum anxiety, it's specifically anxiety about our baby or our job as a mother. It's all the same feelings that come with GAD, but they're all fears about our baby, our baby's health, or if we'll somehow break our baby.

Postpartum depression is talked about a lot more than postpartum anxiety, unfortunately. Postpartum anxiety often gets dismissed as the worry that comes with new motherhood. Many new moms suffer in silence because they're told their hormones need to "level out." Or they're told they need to sleep so they'll feel better. (If you're a new mama and any of this sounds familiar, don't suffer in silence. Please call your doctor.) And again, even if your motherhood journey doesn't include all the hormonal changes from pregnancy, you're not immune to these anxious thoughts either. (Sorry, friend!)

Remember when I mentioned our instincts kicked in as they should have the night of the fire? Well, that's because the threat detection hormone is something we all have, and everyone experiences anxiety in some form or another in their lifetime. It's normal, to a certain extent. It's how our ancestors survived years ago when they found themselves in life-threatening situations. When we are in a stressful scenario, our adrenaline takes over so we can respond, and our brains send the threat detection signal so the body can take action. It's actually a gift from God in that respect.

You have a little almond-shaped part in your brain called the amygdala (not to be confused with Princess Amidala from *Star Wars*—I used to pronounce it wrong). The amygdala is the part of our brains that processes our emotions, and that bad boy is the culprit for the overactive fight-or-flight response. When the amygdala has activated the fight-or-flight response, it begins to pump stress hormones throughout our bodies to get us to respond to the threat in front of us.[6] Of course, when there isn't a real threat in front of us and our amygdalas are still activating on their own, that's when anxiety can become a mental health disorder.

We all know about the common effects of anxiety: the racing mind and heart, the panic attacks, and shortness of breath. But did you know that anxiety can do a lot more to your body? Other effects can include your immune, cardiovascular, and respiratory systems, to name a few.[7] Depression, headaches, irritability, and digestive issues can also be a result of this little chemical imbalance. (Trust me, I know. I had an experience with a gastroenterologist where nothing was found wrong, and now I know it was my anxiety. Also, sorry if that was TMI!)

I know what you're thinking. That was a lot of medical information thrown at you, and maybe you found it boring. But thank you for bearing with me. I know I said I'm not a doctor, but I had to do all this research and we had to go through all this information because I needed to prove a point to you: Anxiety is a medical condition.

It's a chemical imbalance in our brains and in our bodies. It requires a medical diagnosis from a doctor, and it can be treated with medication that can help balance specific chemicals in our brains.

If you're a mama who is reading all this for the first time and you've believed this whole time that it was just in your head or that it was all a spiritual battle—I'm here to tell you, it's a *real* illness of the brain. If you've felt alone with all your worries and fears, well, I'm your new best friend. I'm a mama just like you—battling the fear daily, constantly praying my way through it, and opening my Bible every day.

I'm here to let you know you're not alone, and I'm teaming up with God to help you out.

The Stuff to Think About

- Have you been diagnosed yet? Do you know what type of anxiety disorder you're dealing with? (Maybe you have more than one.)
- Do you know what triggers your anxiety the most? Are these triggers mainly related to motherhood, or have you struggled with them your whole life?

The Stuff to Try Out

- If you're undiagnosed, consider talking to your doctor and doing some research on the different types of anxiety disorders.
- When you start to feel your anxiety heightening, just remember that God is there to comfort you. His comfort will bring you joy. Memorize or write down some verses to cling to when you're starting to feel anxious. (Don't worry, this book is full of them!)

The Truth about It

> When anxiety was great within me,
>   your consolation brought me joy. (Ps. 94:19)

Mommy Sometimes Gets Scared Too

(Feeling: The fear of something bad happening to my kids)

There's a whole lot of fear when you're dealing with anxiety; however, the fear of something bad happening to your kids is probably the biggest fear any mother will ever face. As a Christian mom, you've probably been told to trust God more, or you've heard the famous saying "faith over fear." You've probably been told to "stop worrying so much." I've been told that. A lot. However, being a mom in this day and age is hard because of how crazy and messed up this world is. There are so many things I do not want my kids around or exposed to.

I know; I know. I can't shield them from it all—unless I lock them up in my house forever. (Believe me, I've thought about doing that.) But what I *can* do is rely on God to give me the strength to face these fears. Like, every day. I can turn to Him when the fear sets in, and I can face it all with the strength of God.

If you're a mom of littles or school-aged kids, listen up. I'm going to tell it to you straight. You're not going to like it, and I'm sorry to be the one to tell you this, but here it goes: Your kids are going to move out of your house someday. (I mean probably . . . hopefully, right?)

I know it's painful to think about, but it's true. There will be a day when your kids will move out of your house, and they'll be all on their own. (I'm crying at the thought of that right now!) They may even move thousands of miles away, across the country, as opposed to living just down the street like you'd hope. (No, really, stop it; I'm bawling over here.) Or maybe they've already moved out of your home, and you're consumed with worry every day about their well-being. But truth be told, we're not God, and we can't be everywhere at all times. We can't have our eyes glued to our kids all the time, making sure they don't harm themselves by putting their finger in an electrical socket or running into a wall. If we want to take our joy back in motherhood, we first must face that reality.

Joshua 1:9 reminds us of this: "Have I not commanded you? Be strong and courageous. Do not be afraid; do not be discouraged, for the LORD your God will be with you wherever you go." It's easy to read but hard to remember when we let our minds go off with worry, isn't it? He wants us to remember He is with us wherever we go, and that means He is with our kids too.

We may not be able to be with them wherever they go in life, but God is.

We may not be able to have eyes on them all the time, but God does.

And that brings joy and comfort to this anxious mama's heart.

Hey, PTSD, Come Join My Anxiety

"Is she okay?" I asked in a panic as I watched a nurse beating the back of my two-day-old newborn.

We heard little gasps of air as Adelyn began filling her lungs back up with oxygen.

The nurse looked a little concerned, but not too worried as she replied, "Yeah, she's okay. But if that ever happens again, that's what you need to do. Turn her over on your forearm and just keep beating her back until you hear her breathing again. There's also an emergency cord in the bathroom if you ever need to call the nurses urgently."

We were still in the hospital since Adelyn had slight jaundice. Even though she was born at thirty-seven weeks, she was healthy and at a good weight. We were still trying to get the breastfeeding thing down, and we were using donor milk through a syringe to avoid nipple confusion.

And so, in the wee hours of the morning the next day, Billy was feeding her through a syringe as I was trying to pump and get my milk flowing.

"Is she okay?" It seemed like I was asking that a lot.

He held her up closer to his face, trying to figure out if she was breathing or not. She was drinking the milk from the syringe, but he didn't hear gulps from her swallowing. He wasn't sure if he could hear anything. We thought her skin was beginning to turn purple (we only had the light from the bathroom and bilirubin light), so he turned her over and proceeded to beat her back just like the nurse had shown us.

"Is it working? Is it working?" I cried out to him.

"I. Can't. Tell," he stated in between each beat as he proceeded to beat on her back.

We did not hear gasps of air filling her chest, so I ran into the bathroom and pulled the emergency cord. *There's no alarm sound going off or anything,* I thought. *This isn't fast enough!* So I ran into the hallway. "We need help in here!" I yelled at the nurses sitting at their station.

A whole swarm of nurses came in, and just as they did, Adelyn started breathing. Billy sat there in a state of relief mixed with disbelief at what he just had to do to his baby girl.

I'm sure the nurses thought we were crazy. A doctor came in to hear about what had happened, and she told me to disconnect from the breast pump and get some sleep. They chalked it up to two sleep-deprived parents who couldn't tell if a baby was breathing or not. But they didn't totally dismiss us. The doctor ordered a nurse to be in the room with us every time we fed Adelyn.

Yet again (or sure enough), she stopped breathing again while feeding.

We saw another doctor this time who explained that since Adelyn was a little on the early side, she had not developed her "suck, swallow, breath" coordination. We stayed in the hospital with our baby for a week. So many days that now feel like such a nightmare to me. Adelyn went through occupational therapy, and we had a nurse in the room with us any time we fed her. She was hooked up to an oxygen monitor during that week.

Beep. Beep. Beep.

I would lay there awake just watching the monitor. Listening for those beeps. I can still hear those beeps in my mind even now. You think I was sleep-deprived before? Pssh. That was not how I envisioned the first days of my daughter's life, that's for sure.

When we got home, though, my anxiety became even worse. There was no monitor hooked up to Adelyn telling me she was getting oxygen. There wasn't a nurse to call to perform CPR if Adelyn were to stop breathing. I was constantly checking on her in the middle of the night, and I always wanted Billy in the room with me when I fed her just in case I needed someone to dial 911 while I beat her back. I wouldn't let Grandma or anyone else feed her, which meant no one could come assist me so I could take a nap or a shower or something.

I was experiencing some level of post-traumatic stress disorder (PTSD) on top of the anxiety I already had, a beautiful mixture of fear. I didn't know how to get through all of it (and get some sleep). The worry was taking over, and I began to play out horrifying scenarios in my mind. The what-if-the-paramedics-don't-get-here-in-time type of scenarios.

Have you experienced an event or time in your life that heightened your fears of something bad happening to your children? Whether you've had anxiety your whole life, this type of experience is enough to trigger it, am I right? For me, this experience with Adelyn wasn't quite the tip of the iceberg where my anxiety went from manageable to debilitating. There would be another event in my life that would push my anxiety *way* over the edge.

Okay, God, I'm Afraid but I Trust You

"No, I am not sacrificing Christmas again this year! Not gonna happen, sorry! If God lets COVID come into this house on the day I want to celebrate the birth of His Son, then that's God's plan."

I was getting all fired up about Christmas plans as Billy and I were debating whether we should host family this year. A new variant of COVID-19 was running rampant, and it was the second year of the pandemic. I didn't want to make any more concessions when it came to the holidays. I had "pandemic fatigue," and I also knew I had done everything humanly possible by this point to avoid contracting the virus. I needed to give more over to God. Anxiety had won the war over my mind for so long, so when Christmas 2021 came, I decided fear was not winning. I wanted to celebrate with our family. And so . . .

"Hey, honey," Billy called for me after getting off the phone.

"Yeah?" I asked, already knowing the answer.

"The test was positive."

Thy will be done, Lord.

I said if COVID came for Christmas, it was God's plan and, boy, what a foot-in-mouth moment for me. It's funny how God works like that. He knew the outcome before I had even said those words, and He knew it was finally going to be the big test for me.

The test of trust.

Here's the thing about being a Christian with anxiety while fear overcomes your mind: You know what God says about fear. You hear

Him, and you've memorized all the verses the Bible contains about fear. You know those verses in your heart and soul, and maybe you do trust Him with it all. But there's anxiety's voice in your head. It takes over and makes you do things others would consider crazy as it rationalizes your actions for you. (Just wait until you hear a story about a coffee straw in chapter 11; you'll know what I'm talking about then!) It's important to remember that anxiety's voice and God's voice are not the same. While your brain is telling you, "Hey, there's a threat," God is saying, "Don't be afraid; trust Me. I am always with you."

You may have been told "faith over fear" and felt like you don't have faith because you struggle with fear; but I don't believe that, sorry. I believe you can fully trust God in your soul, but your mind may have a different agenda. Living with anxiety is a constant wrestle between the two. I also believe God can use your anxiety to help you learn to trust Him by having you face your anxiety and fears.

Anxiety may have been in the driver's seat for well over a year with COVID, but when faced with that fear, it was complete trust in God. I surrendered the wheel to God, and it was a constant state of *Thy will be done.*

My son, William, was the first one to show symptoms just two days after Christmas. Adelyn followed right behind, both children spiking a fever of 103 degrees. The whole family was checking on us every day, and as much as they were checking on the kids, I think they were checking more on my mindset to see how I was dealing with it all. And I did just fine. I was filled with His peace. I handed it over to Him and let Him take care of it because that's all you can do when you're forced to face your fears. I truly believe God shaped my pandemic experience to build my trust and faith in Him even more. But that's just my story. Your anxiety and faith journey may be very different.

One of my favorite verses I often recite to myself is Psalm 56:3: "When I am afraid, I put my trust in you." This doesn't mean fear won't exist in my life. It will; I've got anxiety. But when fear does come, it means I can and will put my trust in Him. I may have anxiety—and sometimes it may take over—but that doesn't mean I'm incapable of trusting Him. The truth is my anxiety *needs* me to trust Him. My relationship with God and trusting God is the only way I can function most days. Without Him, I don't know if I'd be able to do simple things like leave the house or sleep.

Perhaps you're not in that part of your faith yet. Maybe you're a new believer, and you're not sure if you trust Him yet. Well, that may very well be the point of your anxiety—to help you learn to trust and rely on Him. And if that's the case, you're going to find that the Bible has a lot to share with you regarding your fear.

God doesn't want us to fear. We know that from His Word. The Bible mentions some variation of the phrase "fear not" 365 times.[1] (Sidenote: In case you try to look up all these verses in the Bible—which I totally did—translations of the original Hebrew and Greek words for "fear not" are what actually appear hundreds of times. Those words can be translated to "do not be afraid," "do not fear," etc.) That's a verse every day for a year, and it's not by accident. Repetition is used in literature to emphasize important points and to stress a certain thought.[2] Even though God doesn't want us to fear and has repeated Himself so many times, He also tells us He will comfort us when we are afraid. Zephaniah 3:17 reads, "With his love, he will calm all your fears" (NLT). He still loves us, despite our fears, and His love will calm these fears.

So if fear is a big issue for you and it's consuming your everyday life to the point that it's stolen your joy, you've got a verse a day to pray on and give you the strength you need to face those fears. And even if those fears take over, or you're one day looking those fears right in the face—put your trust in Him.

That's all He's really looking for from you.

Jesus, This World Is Scary. The End.

Besides the pandemic, 2020 was an anxious year for me. There were so many other newsworthy events that made me anxious. Social unrest. Racial division. Protests and riots. Murder hornets (I bet you forgot about them). Political division. A presidential impeachment trial and an ugly election resulting in the Capitol being attacked.

I. Could. Not. Watch. The. News.

Not to mention there were and are the everyday headlines of kidnappers and sex traffickers lurking about the world. Yeah, that's enough right there to send any mother into an anxiety attack. I don't watch the news anymore. Can't do it. Nope, no way.

The truth is there will always be ugliness in this world until the day Jesus comes again (come, Jesus, come). Satan will continue to corrupt this world every chance he can get. I don't mean to sound depressing over here, but it's the reality of the fallen world in which we live. As mamas in this terrifying world, we have two things to give us hope.

The first is Jesus will return and He will defeat Satan (Rev. 20:10). When He returns, there will be no more pain, no more death, and no more crying. Everything will be made new, and what a glorious day it will be when God will dwell with His people again as He always intended!

The second piece of hope is the knowledge of God's character and His promises. We have a God who is our refuge and strength (Ps. 46:1), who has plans for us (Prov. 19:21), who will fight for us (Deut. 3:22), who is faithful (Ps. 33:4), who is our help and our shield (Ps. 33:20), and who is the God of peace (Judg. 6:24).

Let's take a look at a mama in the Bible who was dealing with fear as her baby's life was literally in danger. Long ago, in the land of Egypt, there was a new king who feared the Israelite people because of how many there were and how powerful they were becoming. He ordered midwives to start killing any Hebrew boys as they were born; but because those midwives feared God, they didn't obey Pharaoh's order. So Pharaoh ordered that every son born to the Hebrews be thrown into the Nile River. This is where we meet Jochebed.

Jochebed was the mother of Moses. I'm sure you've heard of him, and he doesn't need an introduction here, but if not, you can follow along with me in the beginning of the book of Exodus. When Pharaoh ordered all male Hebrew babies to be thrown into the Nile, Jochebed hid her baby for three months. When it became too difficult to hide him anymore, she made a plan to save her baby from being killed. Jochebed got a papyrus basket, which she coated with tar and pitch. (Noah used pitch to coat the inside and outside of the ark to help it float—not really related to my point, but it shows how detailed Jochebed was and how she knew what to do.) She was very precise in how she orchestrated this plan. She laid the baby in the reeds of the river where she knew the basket would not drift away. She then had Moses's sister, Miriam, watch from a distance to see what would happen.

Pharaoh's daughter began to bathe herself in the river and she saw the basket in the reeds. When she saw Moses lying there, crying, she felt sorry for him. Miriam approached Pharaoh's daughter and asked if she should go find a Hebrew woman who was nursing so the baby wouldn't starve, and Pharaoh's daughter consented. Miriam got her mother, Jochebed, to nurse her very own baby. Jochebed didn't get to raise her own baby, but her child's life was spared. Not only did he get to live, but he eventually became the leader who led the Israelites out of slavery from Egypt and wrote the first five books of the Bible. And what did Jochebed do?

She laid her baby in a basket and trusted God to do the rest.

Now, maybe your story doesn't end like Jochebed's. Maybe you've lost your child, and your heart is shattered. Maybe you've had to place your child's life in God's hands, and it didn't result in your baby being spared so your arms are now empty. If that's the case, I can't imagine the pain you've gone through and continue to work through. I can't imagine the fear that has to consume you if you're fearful of something bad happening to your other kids. You may feel like you trusted God, and He didn't deliver. You may feel like you can't trust Him now because of it. You may even doubt that He's real because you're so angry at Him for taking your baby. Those are all valid feelings. I know God is close to the brokenhearted (Ps. 34:18). I pray you look to Him to comfort you in your grief and to be your strength. And I pray for peace for you. Just know that He has your child safely in His arms.

We don't always understand why bad things happen to good people or why God takes a little one too soon, whether it's from an illness or miscarriage. It's hard. It's confusing. I don't have all the answers for it either, but I know He does. He's got the plan, and it never makes sense as it unfolds. Sometimes, it doesn't even make sense until years later or until the very end of our lives when we look back. But we can't live in the fear of tomorrow. We can only hold on to the One who knows the future. Isaiah 41:10 tells us,

> So do not fear, for I am with you;
>> do not be dismayed, for I am your God.
> I will strengthen you and help you;
>> I will uphold you with my righteous right hand.

God may tell us not to be afraid hundreds of times in the Bible, but a lot of the time He'll add "for I am with you" or some sort of comforting reminder that He's right beside us through it all. He's constantly reminding us of His presence. He's not saying we can't be afraid; it's a human emotion we all experience. He's saying when we are afraid, He will strengthen and help us—no matter what.

He's not going anywhere.

Say Hello to Germs, Fires, and Moths

This is probably the point of this chapter where you're thinking, *Okay, Courtney, great encouragement, but I'm still scared!*

Yeah, I'm right there with you. Remember, I didn't claim to be healed or have the magic formula for this. So here's where we get a little practical with the fears we have about our kids or with anything really.

Do you remember the first time your kid did anything for the first time that scared them? Maybe it was their first dentist trip or learning to ride a bike. Maybe you're still in the newborn phase of life; if that's the case, I'll give you an example from my life.

When William was three years old, he had one of his first experiences in a big pool. He was terrified of letting go of Daddy or me. He had a fear of drowning, and he didn't like how deep the pool was. It didn't matter that he had floaties on; it didn't rationalize the fear for him. It didn't matter that we told him we were right there and wouldn't let him drown. He was gripping on for dear life and holding on to his fear.

As parents, when a child has an irrational fear like this, whether it's fear of swimming or fear of a monster in the closet—what do we do? We make them face the fear, and we show them there is nothing to be afraid of. (Unless you're my husband and it's a spider. Yeah, that grown man is afraid of spiders and I'm the spider-killer in the house.)

I want you to think of the same concept here when it comes to your own fears. The only thing we can do to decrease our fears is to face them. And no, I'm not telling you to go walk down a dark alleyway with your kids in tow and see if you'll get mugged. Obviously, don't try to put yourself into a dangerous situation. I would call that a realistic fear anyway, depending on the city you live in. What I'm suggesting is, when it comes to those unrealistic fears—triggered by our friend, anxiety—you face them head-on and expose yourself to them. It's about retraining your brain when it comes to those unrealistic fears and telling yourself there's really nothing to fear.

You'll need to decipher for yourself what's an unrealistic fear. For example, my fear of germs is unrealistic when we're talking about the common cold. Germs are everywhere. So you need to figure out what fears are unrealistic and trigger your heart to start racing. A little tip: You may need help from someone else to determine what's an unrealistic fear. Your anxiety is going to try to convince you all your fears are realistic.

Your fears may not even be related to your kids. They may be something entirely off the charts like a fear of moths. (Yes, that's me; I hate those things!) Reflect on what you are afraid of, create a list, and brainstorm some ways you can start facing them and proving to your anxiety there's nothing to fear.

If you're a mama who is afraid of something bad happening to your kids, start loosening the grip a little bit. Let a babysitter come over who you trust to take the kids off your hands once a week, giving yourself a break. If it's a fear of a house fire, check the burners only once at night instead of three times before you lay your head down to get some sleep. (I say only once because, I'm sorry, but it's still a safety hazard, right? I probably need to work on this one myself.) If it's a fear of germs, start letting your kids go to the germy places. Take them to the park, take them to Walmart, let the baby suck her thumb even though her hands are not washed. Instead of washing their hands every ten minutes, scale it back to right before mealtimes and after they go potty.

I think you catch my drift here. Of course, there will always be more realistic and natural fears we will face as moms. We are human, of course. That's the original intention of the threat detection hormone—to warn us against the real threats of the world. However, when it comes to those fears that are borderline phobias we obsess over because our anxiety is telling us they are life-threatening, we need to rationalize them and overcome them with the strength of God. That's when we'll be able to walk right up to that fear, look it in the eyes, and defeat it.

You know, all David and Goliath style.

The Stuff to Think About

- Can you recall a season in your life when your fear was heightened? How did you handle it? Have your fears intensified since you became a mother? Look at the root cause of your fear and what triggers it.

- Do you feel like trust is a part of your relationship with God? Perhaps you're not there yet in your relationship with God. If that's the case, look to the Bible to learn more about Him. It's hard to have a relationship with someone you don't know, so start with God's Word.

The Stuff to Try Out

- Find some favorite verses about fear (remember, God has a lot to say about fear in the Bible), and memorize them so you can come back to them when you find yourself in a fearful situation. Psalm 56:3 is my favorite, but you'll find hundreds more, so pick your favorite!
- Rationalize your fears or any borderline phobias that you have. Determine which ones are unrealistic and which ones are realistic. Talk this one out with someone else to truly decipher the distinction. Make a list of the unrealistic fears that trigger your anxiety, and start thinking of ways to overcome them. Facing your fears will retrain your brain to think there is nothing to fear.

The Truth about It

When I am afraid, I put my trust in you. (Ps. 56:3)

The Lord is my strength and my shield;
    my heart trusts in him, and he helps me.
My heart leaps for joy,
    and with my song I praise him. (Ps. 28:7)

3

No, Really, My Anxiety Isn't in Control of Me—I Just Have to Control Everything

(Feeling: I get anxious if I feel like I lack control)

"Um, honey . . . I think my water just broke. That's not supposed to happen yet!"

"Are you sure?" Billy responded with a mixture of excitement and disbelief. "Maybe you should call the doctor?"

"Well, no, I'm not sure. It's kinda like I'm leaking, so I don't know," I hollered back at him from the bathroom as I went for my phone.

It wasn't a big gush like you see in the movies. No, it was a little splash and then a slight trickle. Plus, it was my first baby, and I had no clue what was supposed to happen. All I knew was I had just reached the thirty-six-week mark and I didn't even have the car seat installed yet. Otherwise, I had no idea what was going on. I was at the doctor's the day before, and he predicted I would go past forty weeks. (Doctors don't always know everything, okay?)

There was no sign I'd have a baby early; everything was normal and healthy prior to that day.

"Why don't you come into triage, and we'll take a look and see if your water has broken or not," the nurse told me over the phone.

Okay, guess I'd better bring the hospital bag with me just in case then.

I tried not to let my anxiety get the best of me. I tried to remain cool and calm, and I tried to think of any number of other things that could be going on with my body.

I tried to think all those things until I realized . . . I had to pee.

I was on my way back to the waiting room from the bathroom when that gush showed up.

Okay, yeah, my water definitely broke.

Well, of course, they called me back right after that (right about the time I watched the poor hospital worker come up who had to clean my bodily fluids off the floor).

When we got to the triage room, the nurse began taking vitals on me. I tried not to panic about what was happening, so I turned my attention to the television in the room that was playing an episode of *Fixer Upper* (I'm a big fan of Chip and JoJo).

"Are you a little nervous?" the nurse asked me.

"Um . . . yeah, a little," I said with a small smile. *Yeah, no, I'm a lot nervous over here! I already suffer from anxiety, and now we're trying to figure out if I'm having a baby four weeks early!*

"Just try to relax; I'm going to try to take your blood pressure again. Sometimes the first reading is high when you get checked in," she responded.

Okay, relax, I thought as I took a deep breath. *You might be having a baby, but just relax. Don't be anxious.*

Fwoosh.

The blood pressure cuff deflated as the reading came back. I eyed the nurse, looking for a verbalization of what the reading was.

She frowned.

"I'm going to go get the doctor; I'll be right back," she said.

Oh great, that's just what you want to hear. That won't at all send my anxiety through the roof.

"Hey, Courtney. Looks like we might be having a baby today?" the doctor said as he entered the room.

"Yeah, it looks that way," I responded, trying not to cry as all the emotions started to consume me.

He confirmed my water did in fact break and had the nurse take my blood pressure again. To this day, I still couldn't tell you what those blood pressure numbers were. I was never told. All I was told was my blood pressure was high—high enough to be a big deal. High enough to be diagnosed with preeclampsia. High enough to be hooked to an IV of magnesium sulfate to bring my blood pressure down. And since I wasn't having any contractions, they began inducing my labor so we could get my baby out.

Ten hours of labor, four attempts at an epidural (that only half worked), and then . . .

"Baby's heartbeat is dropping. Mom, we need to turn you on your side!" A nurse immediately starts turning me over and placing an oxygen mask around my face to try to supply my baby with more oxygen.

The chaos that ensued after that moment was straight up terrifying. My room was flooded with nurses. It was a nightmare wondering if my baby was okay and what the heck was going on.

But it was completely out of my control.

The car seat that I was still so worried about because it wasn't installed yet. The fact that I didn't get to wrap up things at work before going on maternity leave. The fact that I was having an October baby instead of a November baby like I had planned—like I had wanted.

Nope, none of it was going as planned. None of it was as expected. It was all in God's hands at that moment.

The baby's heart rate stabilized, and after one hour of pushing, there was William—the most precious little baby boy you have ever seen. (I know, every mother thinks that of their own child, but it's true!)

Yeah, Moms Like Control. It's Kind of Our Thing.

William weighed five pounds and nine ounces, and every inch of him was perfect. We avoided the NICU with him; however, he did have jaundice. His weight dropped to an even five pounds by the time we left the hospital. They sent us home with a bilirubin blanket, and we had to return to the hospital every day for a week to check his levels. And since he was early, he was especially sleepy and did not want to breastfeed or latch on properly. So I pumped (and pumped and pumped). It frustrated me that I couldn't nurse my own baby and do something that was supposed to be so natural for a mother. And of course, because of his size, the doctors were stressing the importance of getting his weight up, which put even more stress and anxiety on me to breastfeed. I would eventually go on to exclusively pump because, you know, I could control that. I had better control over my supply because I was the one doing the demanding with how much I would pump.

I took it day by day, step by step. But I had no control over anything else within the first month of William's life, and I didn't like it one bit.

William's birth experience was proof to me that I was not in control.

His birth was God's timing, not mine.

Maybe your journey to motherhood wasn't like this. Maybe it played out like a scene from a movie, or maybe yours was even more terrifying and ended with an emergency C-section or an extensive stay in the NICU. Or maybe you're an adoptive mom, and you went through months and months of infertility; you were unable to control the fact that you couldn't get pregnant, which led you to adopt. Or maybe you're a foster mom, and the child you were fostering was reunited with their biological mother. Maybe you lacked control over the decision and didn't agree with it.

Whatever the case may be for you, whatever motherhood journey you're facing, and whatever experiences you've had in your life, my bet is you can relate with me on this: our anxiety doesn't like the lack of control.

You may want control because you have a fear of the unknown, and thinking about the future makes you anxious. You may feel like you can handle your anxiety better if you're controlling the things that make you anxious. And then there's some who are a little obsessive when it comes to worrying about things and just always need something to worry about (yup, that's totally me). And so, you try to control those worries. When you feel like you lack control, it can make you feel stressed. It can make you irritable and physically exhausted. Plus, we all know how much mothers like to control things—whether you have anxiety or not. We're known for it.

Here are a few lies my anxiety has told me when it comes to controlling the things that make me anxious:

- I need to control how my kids behave when we're out in public and make sure they don't say anything inappropriate or embarrassing. If they do, this defines my job performance as a mom.
- I need to control how the world influences my kids. I need to heavily monitor what they watch on television and keep them far away from social media. Forever. I need to make sure they don't have minds of their own because the world will corrupt their minds and Satan will win if I don't control everything they look at.
- I need to control my kids' every move and watch them 24/7 to make sure they are safe, otherwise bad things will happen to them.
- I need to control who their friends are so I can ensure they're not being taught bad habits or taught to do things I don't want them doing.

Aaah! It's exhausting! I'm overwhelmed after typing out that list. This kind of worry about control takes the joy right out of motherhood, am I right? Yes, there are things we have to monitor and manage, but we can't—and we don't—control every little thing this world will throw at our kids. So why do we do this to ourselves? Well, part of it is because we think it comes with the job description of being a mother. We think if we don't worry about it all, who will?

If you don't make sure Susie gets her homework done, or make sure it's done right, then she may fail the third grade and never graduate high school. If you're not behind the wheel of a car full of kids and there's an accident, then you'd never forgive yourself. You also may think if you don't pay the bills and manage the money, then your family may have financial issues and the water or electricity could get turned off. (And yes, my husband is capable of paying a bill. He's done it. I've let him do it. I know he's a grown man; it's just something I want to control . . . I mean, manage.)

It kind of spirals though, doesn't it? The more we control, the more we want control. It's a vicious cycle that may never end. And you might just have a controlling personality (that's totally fine too), and it might not even be related to your anxiety. Or you may be reading this chapter and wonder what this has to do with anxiety. Maybe you don't experience this part of it at all. But control and fear kind of go hand in hand, and since we just spent a whopping four thousand-some words talking about fear, we need to address the other side of it—control.

But here's the truth: You're never going to be in full control. Never. Not once. Not gonna happen.

All those lies I try to tell myself about my need for control—they're just lies.

God literally has the whole world in His hands.

Once you rest in that fact, you can finally start loosening anxiety's grip over you. Think about it for a moment. The control you're clinging to, my bet is it's making you even more anxious. It's making you more stressed out as you're trying to do it all. It's just giving you more things to worry about.

God has it all, and He sure doesn't want you to worry about it because He's got it covered. Although, I know from years of experience that this truth is sometimes not enough to quiet your anxious thoughts. I know that knowing God's in control and taking care of it all doesn't always calm the racing brain. This is why we need to go to Him when our anxiety tries to convince us we need to be in control.

First Peter 5:7 is a popular verse, and I'm sure you've heard it recited to you by others when you've told them you're anxious. I'm going to type it out again here: "Cast all your anxiety on him because he cares for you."

I seriously debated where I would put that verse in this book or if I'd even include it. It's a verse that's thrown out there so often to those of us who have anxiety as we're told to "just cast your anxiety on Him." But I don't want to focus on the first part of the verse—the "cast all your anxiety" part. I'm sure you already know how to do that. I know you know how to pray, and I'm sure that's the first thing you do when you're anxious. Jesus is our first line of defense with our anxiety. (And if you're a new believer, just an FYI for you, you're gonna need Him to fight your anxiety. It's a whole lot harder without Him; trust me.) So no, I'm not going to look at the first part of the verse. I'm going to look at the last half of it.

"Because he cares for you."

He *loves* you, Mama. The God of the universe. The Creator of everything we see. And He wildly pursues you and is crazy about you. He loves you—unconditionally and with all your flaws—just as you are, anxious brain and all. He cares about your concerns, and He doesn't want to see you gripping on to control for dear life over things He already has covered. He may not be able to pay that water bill (Drats!), but He knows what's up ahead and around the corner.

Let's take a look at another mama in the Bible who had zero control over her life. We find Hagar's story in Genesis 16 and 21.

Hagar found herself in a situation that was not her choice. She was a servant of Sarah, and Sarah was the wife of Abraham, a man whom God promised He would make "into a great nation" (21:18). (At the time, their names were Sarai and Abram. God later changes their names to Sarah and Abraham, which is why, for simplicity's sake, I'm going to refer to them that way.) Sarah was unable to conceive and did not believe God would provide her with a child. God had told Abraham Sarah would get pregnant, but she was pushing ninety years old by this point, and she didn't think it was going to happen. Sarah took matters into her own hands (you could say she tried to control the situation here), and she told her husband to go sleep with her servant and build a family through her. Hagar then became pregnant, and both women grew to despise the other due to their circumstances. And so, Sarah mistreated Hagar. Hagar—pregnant, all alone, and probably terrified—fled into the wilderness.

An angel appeared to her and told her to return to Abraham and Sarah. He promised that her descendants would increase "too numerous to count," and he told her to name her son Ishmael because God listened and heard her misery. Hagar responded, "You are the God who sees me. . . . I have now seen the One who sees me" (Gen. 16:13).

God saw her.

An Egyptian servant who (I'm assuming) didn't want to get pregnant in the first place. A woman who was in a situation she would not have chosen. A woman who had no control whatsoever over her status, her life, her choices—nothing. Zilch. A woman who was mistreated and despised by the very woman she was bound to serve. And God saw her. But that wasn't where her story ended.

In Genesis 21, after Sarah gave birth to her son, Isaac, she couldn't stand the sight of Hagar and Ishmael. She ordered Abraham to send them away. Abraham was apprehensive at first, but God told him to listen to his wife, for He would make a great nation out of Ishmael too. (And yes, by chapter 17 their names have been changed to Sarah and Abraham, so you're all caught up there.)

Abraham sent Hagar and her son away, giving them water and food for their journey. They wandered through the Desert of

Beersheba. When their water had run out, Hagar laid her son under a bush because she could not bear the thought of watching him die. She sobbed in despair. God heard the cries of her son, and an angel appeared to her and said, "What is the matter, Hagar? Do not be afraid; God has heard the boy crying as he lies there. Lift the boy up and take him by the hand, for I will make him into a great nation" (Gen. 21:17–18). God opened Hagar's eyes, and before her was a well of water. God was with Ishmael throughout his whole life as he grew up in the desert, and God took care of both of them.

God sees. God comforts us in our anxiety. God strengthens us when we feel like our life is spiraling out of control and we don't know what to do.

I've got one more story for you about yet another mama in the Bible and how she dealt with the lack of control in her life.

In the book of Ruth, we find a beautiful story of loyalty and faith between two women, Ruth and her mother-in-law, Naomi. Naomi became a widow, and ten years later her two sons would die as well, which would leave Ruth a widow too. Naomi decided to return to her native land of Bethlehem, and she told Ruth and her other daughter-in-law, Orpah, to return home to their families. After some urging, Orpah returned home, but Ruth refused. In Ruth 1:16, Ruth tells Naomi, "Don't urge me to leave you or to turn back from you. Where you go I will go, and where you stay I will stay. Your people will be my people and your God my God."

Ruth had no idea what the future would hold. She had just lost her husband and had no children, which in that society and culture meant she had no status, no protection. I imagine she probably felt like her whole life was spiraling, and she'd lost control of it all. She chose to go with Naomi to a foreign land where she would be an outsider. She chose to follow Naomi's God and remained faithful to Him. And because of that, she was used by God in a big way.

Upon moving to Bethlehem, Ruth met Boaz who was a relative of her late father-in-law. She found favor with him. She and Boaz got married, and she gave birth to Obed who would become the grandfather of King David. Ruth was one of only five women mentioned in the genealogy of Jesus (found in Matt. 1) as she was the great-grandmother to King David whose lineage would eventually lead to Jesus. She had zero control over her life, and yet she went along with the unknown. She followed God's lead, and her story became a part of the Son of God's story.

It might feel impossible for you to relinquish control. It may get you anxious just thinking about it. And maybe it's the little things you're wanting to control; I don't know. However—big or small—it's getting your heart racing just thinking about it all.

And. It's. Consuming. You.

Not to mention taking your joy away from you as well.

Don't worry; we're going to let it go. One thing at a time.

Let It Go (Not to Sound Like *Frozen*, but It's True)

Let's take a look at how we can let go of control.

Make a list of the things you have to control and rationalize those fears. Write down all the things that could happen if you don't control whatever it is. I'm sure you may see things that most definitely need to get done on your list, and if you don't do them, they'll never get done. But I want you to look at why you desire control. Is it a fear of failure? A fear related to your kids? A past experience that's triggering you? What will happen if you don't control it, and is it really something to worry about to the point that you lose sleep over it?

Let it go. Try to think of ways you can let go of your need for control a little bit more so it's not an anxious trigger for you. Maybe it's not a tangible thing you need to control, and maybe it's control of a situation or the future. In that case, instead of sitting there and imagining the worst-case scenarios, surrender it to God. Hand it over, girlfriend. Start small and begin letting go of some little things here and there. Remind yourself the probability of the worst-case outcome is (probably) low, and maybe it's minuscule compared to the weight of control that you're carrying. Push yourself to let go of more and more so you are creating a new habit, one that doesn't require you being in control all the time.

Stop striving for perfection. News flash: Jesus is perfect; not you. You're never going to be perfect all the time. Everything in your life will not and cannot be perfect. Accept that imperfection is okay and learn to let go and loosen your grip on perfection. I promise you will feel much better.

Focus on things within your control. There are some things you can't just hand over to God, of course. He can't pay the bills for you, and He can't physically drive the car for you (well, He could, but He probably won't). So what I want you to focus on is the fact that your fear of lack of control is just that—fear. It's your anxiety telling you that you have to worry about it. It's the obsessiveness taking over and making your brain rule your body.

When you feel like you don't have control, Satan wants you to forget the One who is in control. So out of the list of things you want to control, take a look at the things you actually *can* control. Being in a car crash is not one of them because, unfortunately, there will always be bad drivers on the road or even weather conditions that make driving difficult. This is a situation where you could easily start allowing someone else to drive more and focus on what you can control in the situation, like wearing a seat belt, for instance.

And finally, when you find yourself reverting to old habits of control (and you will), give yourself grace. Don't be so hard on yourself when you do revert, and take it one step at a time. One day at a time, really. I know it's hard. I get it; I really do. But trying to control it all is making your heart race over the little things or the worries of tomorrow, and Jesus has already told us not to "worry about tomorrow, for tomorrow will worry about itself" (Matt. 6:34). The more you try to give up the control, the more you will feel your anxiety lessen.

In the words of Elsa from *Frozen*: "Let it go; let it go. Turn away and slam the door."[1]

The Stuff to Think About

- What areas of your life are you trying to control? Did you go through an anxious season of life that resulted in a need for control? Is fear behind it all? Find the triggers for your control and rationalize the fear behind it all.

The Stuff to Try Out

- Take a look at the areas in your life where you can surrender some control and lessen your anxiety. Focus on the things you can control. If you have to, sing to yourself the "He's Got the Whole World in His Hands" song that you sing to your kids. Say a prayer, meditate on a verse, and fight the urge (as best you can) to hold on to whatever it is that makes you feel in control and less anxious.

The Truth about It

Cast all your anxiety on him because he cares for you. (1 Pet. 5:7)

> In their hearts humans plan their course,
>   but the LORD establishes their steps. (Prov. 16:9)

I Must Not Be Praying Right

(Feeling: Having a mental illness means my faith is weak)

Shortly after I began writing, I published an article with an online lifestyle magazine for women called *Her View From Home* that went in-depth about my debilitating anxiety. I was very proud of the article; it was one of the most vulnerable pieces I had ever written.[1] So, of course, I shared it. I shared it on my blog, my personal Facebook page, and I shared it with family and friends via text, email, you name it. I was so proud! I wanted to shout from the rooftops, "I got published!" Well, instead I received my first hurtful response on social media.

Someone commented on the article and basically said that if I had a close relationship with God, my fear would not be a thing. Instead of being applauded for taking steps to care for my mental health and share my story, I was criticized for not having enough faith. I was a wreck—curled up in my husband's arms, bawling my eyes out kind of a mess. I read my Bible every night, went to church every Sunday, prayed every day, and yet, I was told if I had faith, my anxiety would be nonexistent. *Poof,* it wouldn't exist.

I'll be honest, the interaction with this person devastated me but also fueled my fire to write this book. I thought, *How many other women have been told something like this from strangers, family members, friends, or even Christian counselors and pastors? How many are out there struggling with fear and are praying for God to take it all away? How many are beating themselves up, thinking their fear means they don't believe enough?* If this is you, well then, I'm truly sorry. But I'm happy you found this book, because I'm here to tell you that having anxiety doesn't make you less of a Christian.

We've all heard the story of Eve taking a bite into that darn fruit. The entrance of sin into the world left us living a cursed life, and our bodies will all eventually fail us in one way or another. Women will endure the pains of labor to bring life into this world (thanks a lot, Eve). Illness will befall us, be it blindness, disease, cancer, etc. Our earthly bodies are perishable, broken, and weak; it's our imperishable, strong, resurrected bodies that will be raised in glory for all eternity with our Father (1 Cor. 15:42–44). If we're experiencing anxiety because of a mental illness, our faith is not weak—our body is. Remember, all the fun stuff we went over in chapter 1 proved that point!

Throughout the Bible, we see biblical figures who experienced feelings of depression, anxiety, despair, and loneliness. King David was described as a man after God's own heart (1 Sam. 13:14), and he struggled with his mental health. Just think about that for a minute. One of God's most beloved men was so devoted to the Lord, but he *still* battled these thoughts and issues—just like us. (See for yourself in Psalm 13 where David describes feelings of depression. In Psalm 139:23 he talks about being anxious.)

David wasn't the only one who wrestled with depression and anxiety. The prophets Elijah and Jeremiah fought feelings of depression (we'll talk about them later). Then there's Jonah who had just survived being swallowed by a fish, but in his anger, tells God he wishes he were dead (Jon. 4:3). God comforted all of them in their despair and loneliness. He didn't shun them for having little faith or not trusting Him enough. Instead, He cared and provided for them through it all.

I can guarantee you one thing: God isn't going to shun you like the people who've told you that you don't have enough faith. He knows your heart and fears, and He's kept record of it all. Psalm 56:8 tells us, "You keep track of all my sorrows. You have collected all my tears in your bottle. You have recorded each one in your book" (NLT). There's no pain and there are no tears we've shed that He doesn't already know about.

He isn't going to turn His back on you.

His love for you endures forever (Ps. 136).

If I Have Anxiety, Am I a Sinner?

(Warning: We're going to start with the big, loaded question. Spoiler alert: I don't have an answer, but stick with me. I'm sure I'll still prove a point.)

I remember when I first started reading Christian books about anxiety. A lot of them were the how-to kind of books where *boom*—you're healed. I found one book I just couldn't force myself to finish. The book referred to anxiety as sinful. I wanted to curl up in a ball and eat a container of mint chocolate chip ice cream while I cried out, "Why, God, why me?" I couldn't understand how a God who loved me so much would tell me I've sinned because there was something wrong with my brain. I imagined myself arriving at the pearly white gates of heaven and being turned away. I imagined God saying, "Yeah, no, you had too many panic attacks in your life, so you can't enter."

It's the biggest question on the mind of any believer who suffers from any kind of mental illness: Am I a sinner?

I can't answer it fully, my friend, because I'm not God. (And remember, He's the only One who gets to judge us in the end.) I will, however, attempt to bring some of my own insight to the conversation. But remember, I'm not a pastor, and I don't have a degree in biblical studies. We're just two mamas talking about faith and anxiety here.

Let's look at the definition of sin. *Merriam-Webster* defines *sin* as a "transgression of the law of God," or "a vitiated state of human nature in which the self is estranged from God."[2] We all know the "transgression of the law of God" is an act against His commandments (and there isn't a commandant that states, "Thou shall not be anxious"). The self estranged from God is the separation sin causes between us and God, even if for a moment. Now, I don't know about you, but I feel closer to God when I'm anxious. I cling to Him more when my heart starts racing.

There's the dictionary's definition of sin, but do you remember the definition of anxiety? There's anxiety that's an emotional response to our situations, it's a normal human emotion, and it's an instinctual survival response we all possess. Then there are anxiety disorders, which can be caused by a chemical imbalance in your brain, whether it's a biological imbalance or a traumatic experience that's triggered the imbalance. That kind of anxiety is excessive, unrealistic, and persistent, and interferes with daily life. That kind of anxiety gives you adrenaline over the smallest things (but makes them a big deal—so big that you could spend hours obsessing over them at 1:00 a.m.). That kind of anxiety is an issue with your brain, not your faith.

Here's the way I see it: There are other medical conditions out there such as cancer, and I know having cancer isn't a sin. So I can't imagine having an anxiety disorder is. Again, I don't have a straight answer for whether anxiety is a sin. Only God knows the answer.

Either way, the Bible tells us we are all sinners (Rom. 3:23). Even if my anxiety is not a sin, I've already sinned in some way throughout my lifetime. We all have, so there is no need to hide from that fact. That's why God sent His Son, Jesus Christ, to become sin for us and set us right with Him (2 Cor. 5:21). His sacrifice on the cross paid the debt we could not pay, reconciled us with our Creator, and paved the way for redemption and eternity with Him. That's the Good News we Christians believe, right (can I get an amen)?

While I'm unable to give you a straight answer to this loaded question, I will leave you with a few verses I've found that may help:

And I am convinced that nothing can ever separate us from God's love. Neither death nor life, neither angels nor demons, neither our fears for today nor our worries about tomorrow—not even the powers of hell can separate us from God's love. (Rom. 8:38 NLT)

Highlight "neither our fears for today nor our worries about tomorrow." Underline it, and store that baby in your memory.

As he went along, he saw a man blind from birth. His disciples asked him, "Rabbi, who sinned, this man or his parents, that he was born blind?"
    "Neither this man nor his parents sinned," said Jesus, "but this happened so that the works of God might be displayed in him." (John 9:1–3)

In the story of Jesus healing a blind man, the blind man wasn't being punished because of his sins. Instead, his suffering could display the works of God.

If our hearts condemn us, we know that God is greater than our hearts, and he knows everything. (1 John 3:20)

You may beat yourself up about your anxiety. You may condemn yourself as a sinner, but God knows your heart. I love how The Message puts it: "For God is greater than our worried hearts and knows more about us than we do ourselves."

Google Doesn't Have All the Answers

Where did the stigma come from? Why do Christians believe if you suffer from anxiety (or really any mental illness) it means something's wrong with your prayer life or your faith in general?

Google it.

No, I'm serious. If you google "What does God say about anxiety?" word-for-word, what do you come up with? (Go ahead and do it, I'll wait.)

Here's what popped up when I googled it: "Do not be anxious about anything, but in every situation, by prayer and petition, with thanksgiving, present your requests to God" (Phil. 4:6). And the other verse that came up right away was "for God gave us a spirit not of fear but of power and love and self-control" (2 Tim. 1:7 ESV). You've heard these two verses, right? Other believers have quoted them to you, and you've referred back to them when your anxiety was the highest, I'm sure. You've probably felt some shame because God says, "Don't be anxious about anything," and that He "didn't give you a spirit of fear." Yeah, those two chunks right there would make you feel some shame for your anxiety. However, when it comes to reading the Bible, context is everything. We're going to debunk this "Christians can't have anxiety" stigma, one verse at a time.

Let's look at that popular Philippians verse first. The apostle Paul was writing a letter to the church in Philippi while he was imprisoned. Although he was in jail, the letter was pretty positive, and Paul seemed to have had a close relationship with the church. At the end of Philippians 2, Paul wrote that he was sending his "co-worker," Epaphroditus (yeah, I can't pronounce that either), to deliver his letter (v. 25). The Philippians had sent Epaphroditus to Paul as their messenger to minister to Paul's needs. As Paul was preparing to send him back, he wrote, "Therefore I am all the more eager to send him, so that when you see him again you may be glad and I may have less *anxiety*" (v. 28, emphasis added).

Yeah, you just read that right.

Paul said he was experiencing anxiety, but that wasn't the only time he experienced fear. When he traveled to Corinth, he wrote in 1 Corinthians 2:3 that he came to Corinth in "weakness with great fear and trembling." He was afraid his preaching ability might be inadequate. While he was in Corinth, the Lord appeared to him in a vision and told him, "Do not be afraid; keep on speaking, do not be silent" (Acts 18:9). Even with all Paul's fear, he stayed in Corinth for a year and a half, and the Lord was with him.

I could dig even deeper into Paul's anxiety, but here's the point: Paul—the guy who was pivotal in writing the New Testament and launching the early church—was a little bit of a worrier.

You may be thinking, *But Paul wrote, "Do not be anxious about anything" (Phil. 4:6), so does that mean he's a hypocrite?* No! It means he's human. And it also means a lot of Christians will read Philippians 4:6 and only see, hear, or retain the "Do not be anxious about anything." Period. They stop right there. But if they kept going, they would read, "but in every situation, by prayer and petition, with thanksgiving, present your requests to God." If they went even further into verse 7, Paul continued saying, "And the peace of God, which transcends all understanding, will guard your hearts and your minds in Christ Jesus."

Do not be anxious about anything, *but* when you are anxious, take your prayers to God with thanksgiving. The peace of God will then guard your hearts and your minds; and His peace transcends all understanding. Paul wasn't saying that to meet the criteria of being a Christian, you're not supposed to be anxious ever; he himself was anxious. He was just giving direction on what to do when you are anxious, and he was offering reassurance that God's peace is like nothing of this world. God will guard our hearts and minds.

Now, on to that 2 Timothy verse.

Paul also authored this verse, and he was writing to his fellow coworker Timothy. Timothy and Paul had a very personal relationship; Paul compared his relationship to Timothy to a father-son relationship. Second Timothy was written during Paul's last imprisonment, and he was expecting to be put to death soon, so you can imagine writing these words to someone you have a deep personal relationship with—you're going to encourage them as you're nearing the end of your life. Paul writes in 2 Timothy 1:6, "For this reason I remind you to fan into flame the gift of God, which is in you through the laying on of my hands." He then continues in verse 7, "For the Spirit God gave us does not make us *timid*, but gives us power, love and self-discipline." I'm adding emphasis because the first time we looked at this verse, it was from a different translation, and "timid" was "fear."

Paul was urging Timothy not to be shy, timid, or afraid to use the gifts God had given him. The Message reads, "And the special gift of ministry you received when I laid hands on you and prayed—keep that ablaze! God doesn't want us to be shy with his gifts, but bold and loving and sensible." (See, context is important!) Little Greek lesson here: The word "spirit" in this verse is the Greek word *pneuma*, which means "wind, breath, spirit,"[3] and Paul was referring to the Holy Spirit who lives within us. Paul was telling Timothy that the Spirit would give him the power to stomp out any fears he was facing.

There's another verse I want to take a look at to help me prove my point. When Jesus was tested by an expert in the Law about what must be done to inherit eternal life, Jesus answered the question with another question (as He often did). We see the man's response, reciting from the Law in Luke 10:27, "'Love the Lord your God with all your *heart* and with all your *soul* and with all your strength and with all your *mind*'; and, 'Love your neighbor as yourself.'" (I've emphasized those words; you see where I'm going with this?) Heart, soul, and mind—three different things here. He didn't just say, "Love God with all of your heart"; no, this verse describes how we humans have multiple layers. We're complex. End of story. To even further prove my point, when the disciples kept falling asleep after Jesus had asked them to pray with Him in Matthew 26:41, Jesus told them, "The spirit is willing, but the flesh is weak." Your spirit and your flesh are two different things.

The point I'm trying to make in all of this is my spirit can be willing and trust Jesus with my all, but my mind (or flesh) is weak. And the Holy Spirit who dwells within me is not one of fear or timidity. He can't be shaken. But my brain—the organ incapsulated by my skull—tells me there's something to fear. The mental illness of my brain is fully capable of fear. Unfortunately, my brain senses danger, even if there's nothing to be afraid of. My soul and my flesh (or in this case, my brain) are two separate things.

Your soul and spirit can stand firm in your faith, but your body can still be ... well, anxious.

Thankfully, we've been given the gift of God's Spirit who (even if momentarily) can shut down those fears and guard our minds with the peace of God.

Hey, Jesus, I Need You

So where's the silver lining in all of this? It's just miserable and unending worry, right? You're probably thinking, *Why do I have anxiety? What's the whole point of all this if it's not a sign of weak faith? Why, God; why me?* Friend, we're going to shift our perspective here just a bit.

Let's look at the Israelites for a moment. They spent four hundred and thirty years in slavery waiting for God to save them. I'm sure there were moments they felt betrayed because He promised them the promised land and then didn't deliver it (at least not yet). I'm sure they had times they thought He had abandoned them or maybe that He didn't even exist. God could've saved them at any moment. He could've snapped His fingers, destroyed the Egyptians, and taken away all their suffering right then and there. But He didn't. And maybe it's because God knew if He saved them right away, they wouldn't have such a strong faith in Him. Putting them through all of that most likely made them stronger in their faith. God's plans can test us, and within those tests, they strengthen us and (hopefully) grow us closer to Him.

We've all gone through seasons of difficult trials, or we've been handed something that makes life, well, hard. Whether you turned to Him or not during that time, it doesn't change the fact that He wanted you to rely on Him to get you through it. Because of my anxiety, I rely on Him *more*. I need Scripture to remind me what He says about fear. I need prayer to help me cope with the everyday anxiousness I feel. I need the power of the Holy Spirit to remind me I'm not alone; I can conquer my anxiety (even if temporarily) because He strengthens me.

So to those who tell you your faith is weak if you have anxiety, I say, "No, my faith is *stronger* because I have anxiety."

I'll be honest, though; my faith has not always been strong. Jesus and I—we've not always had the relationship we do now. I've turned away from Him, and gosh, did it make me feel weak.

Growing up, I was Jesus's girl. You name it, I did it all for my Jesus. Serving in church, youth group, teaching Sunday school at the age of thirteen. I even wanted to be a nun when I was eight. (At the time, I believed that was the only job for a woman within the church.) But a lot changed when I started struggling with depression in my early teenage years. Satan tried to tell me I needed to put a period in my story and be done with it all. (Thank You, Lord, for not letting that happen.) Going through all of that at such a young age—feeling so low and hopeless—made me feel far away from my Jesus. Depression made it harder to follow God. I felt like such a sinner for thinking those thoughts. I felt so unworthy of His love and this life. I felt selfish and ungrateful and, honestly, I didn't know how to get back to Him. I'd love to tell you my depression drove me straight into His arms . . . but it didn't.

It's not like I stopped believing in Him. We just didn't have the take-up-your-cross-and-follow-Me relationship. It was more of a yeah-maybe-I'll-see-You-at-Easter-and-Christmas relationship. It was years of not turning to my Jesus in the middle of struggle. Years of occasionally going to church maybe twice a year (if that). Years of my Bible sitting on the shelf collecting dust. Years of trying to appear put together like I could do it all. Well, I couldn't. I can't.

You may remember that Adelyn's first week of life was stressful and anxiety-filled for me. It didn't help that we had spent a week in the hospital with her, and it also didn't help that she was born in January at the height of influenza and RSV season. That week in the pediatric unit with her we heard the cries and coughs of the children in the rooms next to us. I never wanted to go outside with Adelyn for fear she'd catch a cold. It was too freezing cold to go anywhere with a newborn anyway. As a result of the isolation and the mixture of PTSD and anxiety I had with her, I also started feeling my depression creep back in. That pit of depression was trying to pull me back down, and I needed someone to lift me back up.

Then one day, I felt this nudge. I had subtly felt these nudges for a couple months prior. I had asked for the chaplain in the hospital to bless Adelyn after she was born and asked if I could receive Communion. The nudges had been there, but this time it felt more like a shove. I felt the nudge to read the book *The Purpose Driven Life* by Rick Warren. I had owned this book for years, and it had managed to move with me seven times and across the country without ever being put in the Goodwill pile. But I'd never opened it. It just sat there on my bookshelf, covered in dust much like my Bible. I knew I needed to get out of this depressive funk, and I didn't know what else to do. *Might as well give it a try*, I thought.

I read the book and fell in love with it. I won't spoil it for you, but it's a book you may want to read if you haven't already. After I finished that book, I needed something else to read, so I went to the other dusty book on the shelf: the Holy Bible.

I found the very verses I needed to give me some hope through my depression. I started doing Bible studies and digging deeper into His Word. I felt as though the God I thought I knew all those years ago really wasn't God's character at all. I wanted to learn even more about Him. I wanted—no, needed—more of my Jesus. My illness had returned, the very illness that drove a wedge between us before; but this time, He was my strength and comfort through it all.

Isn't that something beautiful? The very thing—my depression—that kept me feeling distant from Him all those years was the one thing that made me seek Him out again. I found His grace and no longer felt ashamed of my mental illness. I was not yet healed but, through Him, I found the strength to keep going every day. He led me to start writing as a way of therapy, and He led me to share my story with others so that I could help you too.

That's the amazing truth to it all. Sin, illnesses, and our past don't keep us from Him. That's why He came and died for our sins, right? Because He didn't want to be separated from us any longer. He wants a relationship with us. He wants us to run to Him when life is just too darn hard.

God wants to comfort and strengthen you. *He just wants you.* That's all, my friend. If your anxiety makes you feel like you have little faith—because why would a God who heals the deaf and blind let you suffer if you're a true believer—I'm here to tell you He has never left your side. Not once.

Jesus never said we wouldn't have suffering in this world. In fact, He said we would. But He told us to take heart because He has overcome this world (John 16:33). James puts it this way in James 1:2–4:

Consider it *pure joy,* my brothers and sisters, whenever you face trials of many kinds, because you know that the testing of your faith produces perseverance. Let perseverance finish its work so that you may be mature and complete, not lacking anything. (Emphasis added; I love highlighting any part of a verse with the word "joy" in it!)

James goes on in verse 12 to say, "Blessed is the one who perseveres under trial because, having stood the test, that person will receive the crown of life that the Lord has promised to those who love him."

The way I see it, anxiety is my trial in this world, and I'm going to persevere through it with faith. I'm going to pray with my racing mind, and I'm going to worship Him with my racing heart. I'm going to cling to my Bible when my anxiety gets going, and I'm going to continue keeping my eyes on Jesus.

My anxiety keeps me closer to Him.
And being close to Him brings me great joy.

The Stuff to Think About

- Have you ever had someone tell you to "pray more" or "have more faith" when it comes to your anxiety? How did that make you feel? How did you respond? Do you think their response was because they were uneducated about anxiety as a mental health disorder? Consider how you may respond to someone in the future who makes you feel like you have weak faith. Perhaps, next time, you can educate them and gently break the stigma around anxiety.

- Does your anxiety keep you closer to God? Do you think that may be the reason for it all? If you're not feeling very close to Him, use your anxiety as a way to build your relationship and rely on Him more.

The Stuff to Try Out

- An anxiety disorder is not a result of weak faith, but the result of an imperfect brain. If you've never looked at it that way, I want you to start. Accept the illness of your brain and free yourself from feeling like a failed Christian.

The Truth about It

And I am convinced that nothing can ever separate us from God's love. Neither death nor life, neither angels nor demons, neither our fears for today nor our worries about tomorrow—not even the powers of hell can separate us from God's love. (Rom. 8:38 NLT)

Consider it pure joy, my brothers and sisters, whenever you face trials of many kinds, because you know that the testing of your faith produces perseverance. Let perseverance finish its work so that you may be mature and complete, not lacking anything. (James 1:2–4)

#EpicMomFail

(Feeling: My anxiety makes me feel like a failure)

"Stop crying; I can't take it! Please, both of you just stop it!"

I snapped.

My toddler was throwing a tantrum about something and my six-month-old was screaming her head off because she was hungry (and sleepy and teething and probably needing a diaper change too). I couldn't handle how hard this day was. Really, I couldn't handle how hard the last six months had been. I was struggling with depression, and I wasn't ready to admit it yet. My anxiety was jumpy, and the smallest things were setting it off.

My heart started racing as the screaming persisted from Adelyn.

My chest was getting tight as I felt myself getting pulled in several directions by William.

My mind was already distracted by other things, and I felt overwhelmed by it all.

"No, seriously, buddy, leave Mommy alone for a bit. Mommy needs a time-out."

Yup, I put myself in a time-out. The mom rage had unleashed, and the tears started streaming from my eyes as the mom guilt filled me. *There's two of them now*, I thought. *I'm outnumbered, and I can't do this.*

I was a hot mess of mental illness and motherhood.

So I did what every mother does when it's all too much for her: I curled up on the floor of my bedroom and started crying to myself ... and I prayed. *Lord, please help me transition to being a mama of two. It's harder than I thought it would be, that's for sure. I pray You will help me with my depression and anxiety, and I also pray You will help me to be more patient with my kids. Please help me through all of this. I pray in Jesus's name, amen.*

Of course, William followed me into the bedroom because children follow Mommy everywhere. He didn't say anything to me; he just walked over to my nightstand, picked up a book, and handed it to me. It was a book I'd never opened before in my life. My friend had bought it for me, and there it sat on my nightstand, unopened. The book was titled *Promises from God's Word*, and it was filled with Bible verses for all sorts of tribulations and emotions. I opened this little, pink, pocket-sized book to the first page. The first section of the book was entitled "Help."

Help.

(Cue more crying from me.)

Help—that was the word that stood out to me as I was sitting on the floor, praying. God was pointing me to His Word to find the help I needed. And I know this was a clear message from God because what child sees his mom crying then goes and hands her a book he's never even seen her open? It was no accident or coincidence. God was providing me the help I needed, and that help was Him.

He has helped me through it all.

He *does* help me every day.

I think all moms have moments when they're not too proud of themselves. Moments when they lose their temper and snap at their kids. Moments when they are filled with guilt because instead of offering up grace and patience, they turned into that angry mom who yells at her kids in the front yard for the whole neighborhood to hear. And if a mom says she's never lost her cool with her kids, I'm sorry, but she's gotta be lying.

I'm going to venture a guess here that these moments happen frequently for you. They may not happen more than the average mom, but I imagine your anxiety makes you snap and makes you more irritable than you would like. Irritableness is common with anxiety because we don't sleep well, and when we feel overwhelmed, our threat detection gets turned on. So I'm going to guess you know what I'm talking about, and you've felt like the "snappy mom." And I'm also going to assume, as a result, you feel like you're the world's worst mom ever. Really doesn't take much to assume that fact. We all feel like #WorstMomEver at some point. (Okay, every day.)

And that's exactly what Satan wants you to believe.

He wants you to cling to the idea that your anxiety makes you a horrible mom, wife, friend, daughter, and overall human being. He wants you to think every night of all the ways you failed as a mom that day. He wants you to believe you're ruining your kids. He wants you to keep fixating on what makes you feel like a bad mom, to the point that you forget what makes you a great mom.

Satan. Is. A. Liar.

In John 8:44, Jesus (speaking about Satan) says, "When he lies, he speaks his native language, for he is a liar and the father of lies."

Don't believe the father of lies.

Here's your reminder because you need to hear it: You're a great mom.

Write it down on a sticky note for the front of the fridge because you need to remember it. You might not have heard it today, or it might have been a while since you heard it last, but you are a great mom. You may worry and obsess. You may overthink and have panic attacks. You may lose sleep because you're filled with fear, but you're still a great mom. You still love those kids with all you've got, and I'm sure they know how hard you try. But you cannot, and I do mean *cannot*, let Satan get to you with the lie that because you have anxiety, you are a failure and a horrible mama. Don't let him win. Don't let your anxiety define your job performance as a mother either.

I think, as moms, we feel personally responsible for our kids' happiness. We think it's all on our shoulders for how they'll turn out. And when we feel our anxiety spiraling, we naturally blame ourselves when we snap over the little things, like when they start whining about wanting more fruit snacks. There are a lot of demands on our shoulders every day and managing it all can lead to stress, which can lead to (even more) anxiety. I get it; it's hard!

The prophet Elijah knew something about it all becoming too much for him. In 1 Kings 19, after the massacre of false prophets of Baal, Elijah found his life being threatened. He ran because of fear and failure. He journeyed into the wilderness, and I'm sure he felt lonely in all he was trying to accomplish, like he was the only real prophet left. I'm sure he felt inadequate. I'm sure he felt overwhelmed by it all. But just as he was praying to God to take his life (another example of depression here), how do you suppose God responded?

An angel appeared, fed him, and allowed him to rest.

The angel then appeared a second time and fed Elijah again. Elijah then encounters God who gave him further instructions on what to do next.

God comforted Elijah in his feelings of fear and failure.

God could've said, "Hey, get over this and move on because I need you to do what I've called you to do." No, He didn't respond like that. He didn't dismiss Elijah's feelings as being silly or tell Elijah he needed to suck it up and stop worrying so much. God comforted him in his fear and cared for him. He provided for him, and after Elijah recovered and felt better, God sent him back to work. As you can see from Elijah, God will meet us in our overwhelmed state and give us the help we need to keep going.

So what can we do when our anxiety is making us feel irritable and snappy?

I have a few suggestions.

Mommy needs a time-out. We know we all need breaks in motherhood, but they are hard to come by. We feel guilty for asking for a salon day or something. Forget a salon day; we'd love to leave the kids to their own devices and do a girls' weekend with a bunch of friends. Regular breaks are important for moms. The end. However, when we're in a moment of feeling on edge and our anxiety is making us irritable, a simple time-out may help. Children need time-outs or quiet time when they're overstimulated or acting out, and we could benefit from this too. Locking ourselves in the bathroom (which I know we know how to do) and taking a little breather from our kids can help us to calm ourselves down.

Breathe—literally. It helps. Mothers of littles may be familiar with *Daniel Tiger's Neighborhood*. Imagine Mom Tiger singing to us, "When you feel so mad that you want to roar, take a deep breath and count to four."[1] The concept literally works, not just for our kids but for us too. We may have heard of "breath prayers," which are a combination of breathing techniques and prayer. (Thank you to my counselor for this suggestion.) This is when science and the Bible meet up to defeat anxiety. Let me give an example from my favorite verse. Take a deep inhale and whisper or think, "When I am afraid . . ." and then exhale, "I put my trust in You." We can recite any passage of Scripture that speaks to us, but breathing techniques are scientifically proven to calm anxiety. When we're taking those deep breaths, we're sending a message to our brains that says, "Hey, anxiety, there's no threat around, so you can just chill out."[2] There are several breathing techniques we can use for anxiety (google it), but I've become a big fan of the breath prayers and using Scripture with them.

Pray, of course. Now that we've gotten ourselves to a secluded time-out spot and we've taken a breather, we're going to pray this prayer.

Dear God, hey. It's me, anxious mama over here. I'm having a hard time right now with my anxiety. Can You help me? My kids are getting on my nerves, and I can feel my anxiety ramping up. My heart is racing, and it feels like it's going to pound right out of my chest. Please, Lord, help me. Help me to give my kids the same grace You give me every day. Please help me rest this anxious heart of mine and slow down this anxious mind. Thank You for being my strength when the days are hard and my kids are difficult. I pray You help me not be so hard on myself too. I pray in Jesus's name, amen.

And finally, when we've had a hard day, turn to a friend for some encouragement. I'll be said friend for the purpose of this moment.

Hey friend, you're not a bad mom for having anxiety. Yes, your anxiety makes you do things you are not proud of, and it may make you anxious over the littlest things, but you are still a good mom. You're the exact mom God wanted for those kiddos, and He knew what He was doing when He created you. Maybe caring too much is exactly what those kids need. Maybe snapping some days causes you to love them even harder on other days, and those are the days your kids will remember when they are all grown up. Maybe your kids will look at you and see all the struggles you dealt with and how it shaped them in their future, or maybe they'll admire you even more for your strength.

Give yourself a little bit of grace, Mama. You are doing God's work, and you're doing it with anxiety. You may have snapped today or had a bad day, but I know you'll get back up and try again tomorrow. Take a deep breath when the anxiety sets in, say a little prayer, and get back to it. You've got this, my friend.

Don't Let Comparison Steal Your Joy

We've talked about mom guilt, so let's move on to the other thing moms are notorious for—comparison. (And how our anxiety feeds off it.)

My sister and I had our boys ten days apart, which was fun because I'd have someone to text in the middle of the night when we were both awake feeding newborns or pumping. However, as the years have gone on, we've had a lot of conversations that sound something like this:

"Oh, wow! You're letting him drink juice already?"

"Are you still breastfeeding? I don't think I can keep up with this anymore."

"He's talking already! I can't even get mine to say 'Mama.'"

"Oh, really, you haven't started potty training yet? Mine's already pooping on the potty!"

"What kind of discipline methods are you using? I know I don't want to spank my kids, but I can't seem to get time-outs to work."

"That kid can count to twenty already! Any time I try to sit down with mine and go through our ABCs, I can't get him to concentrate long enough."

We've swapped stories like this a lot and still do from time to time. Don't get me wrong, there's nothing wrong with seeking advice from other moms. This was my sister's second kid and my first, so I had no clue what I was doing. However, what tended to happen was when her parenting decisions would differ from mine or from what my gut was telling me to do (and vice versa), I'd compare myself to her as a mother.

We know motherhood can heighten anxiety when it comes to fear and worry, but there is so much more that can create anxiety when it comes to being a mom. We constantly question whether we are doing things right, and that never stops. Even if we have more children, our kids are entering new, uncharted territory, and we have no idea what's going on. It's decision after decision—all day, every day—and obsessing over what the ramifications will be if we make the wrong choice. Then there's the world of social media, which only makes it worse because we start comparing ourselves to other moms through their Instagram grids. Moms we've never even met in person but hey, she looks more put together and like she's a better mom than me. Then enters *more* mom guilt.

Nobody ever warns you about how much you'll beat yourself up over your job performance as a mother. I look at all these moms who have a calendar full of activities for their kids and the moms who have arts and crafts all laid out every day, and then thoughts start racing through my head: I'm not a good mom, I'm a lazy mom who does nothing with my kids, my kids are going to be behind in school because I haven't taught them their ABCs yet, and on and on. Cue my anxiety over my job as a mother.

If you're sitting there thinking, *Yuh-uh, I can relate to all of this!* Well, we're going to stop worrying about what others are doing and take God's advice here.

Galatians 6:4–5 reads, "Each one should test their own actions. Then they can take pride in themselves alone, without comparing themselves to someone else, for each one should carry their own load." Don't let comparison raise your anxiety; you don't know the load someone else is carrying. We're all on different motherhood journeys with different backgrounds and life experiences, and we all have different family situations and values we want to instill in our children. You know what's best for *your* family.

When you start looking at what the rest of the world is doing or the mama who's doing it different than you—it's robbing you of your joy. Let her do her thing and you do yours.

I bet you anything you'll feel less mom guilt, and you'll find some peace for your anxiety.

One Minute, Please—I'm Overthinking

"So what do you think about that?" he asked me.

I was in my own little world called Courtney's Brain, and Billy was pulling me back into the present. "I'm sorry, what was the question?" I asked.

"Never mind, you obviously don't care," he responded, and it was like a gut punch. I immediately felt guilty for not paying attention to him when he was talking.

"No, seriously, can you just repeat it? I'm sorry, I was just thinking about something else, but I'm listening now."

"Just forget it," he said.

Ugh.

My heart sank. I couldn't tell you where my mind was, but it was gone, and I was unable to recall what he had just said. The racing thoughts and inability to focus were making it difficult to have a conversation with him. I began to get upset that he wouldn't repeat the question. I apologized, so why wouldn't he just repeat himself for me and we could continue our conversation? *So annoying, it's not that hard to just repeat it*, I thought.

But this is not a rare occurrence for us. In fact, this can happen nightly if my brain is going off on something else. Gosh, it sure makes me feel horrible when I see how it plays out and how it can affect my relationships. I feel like a horrible wife. I feel like a bad mom. I feel like an inadequate friend, sister, daughter—you name it.

I even find myself wandering off in a tailspin in the middle of my prayers. (Yeah, I'm going to be 100 percent honest with you here.) I'll be in the middle of a prayer and, all of the sudden, something I'm having a conversation with God about becomes a run-on sentence or brain dump. I find myself apologizing to God for getting off topic. Sometimes it can take me forever to get a prayer finished because of how many times I lose track and let my brain go off. I'm sure God is thinking, "Seriously, Courtney, could you just finish this prayer? Go to sleep already! I've got other things to do!" I know He's a forgiving God, and He knows how lousy I feel every time I fail to put my focus completely on Him.

It makes me feel like my inability to get a prayer complete in a timely manner makes me a crummy Christian, like there must be other Christians who God loves more because their prayers are prettier and not some random, jumbled, totally off topic mess.

Another lie, my friend. Don't buy into that one. Your prayers may not always be pretty, but your heart is there, and God knows your heart. We know that. The end.

Back to the inability to focus, though. (See! I even trailed off topic right there!) Let me paint a picture for you. Back in my former career life, if you had walked into my office, you would've found a desk covered in a heaping mess of papers. I was notorious for multitasking, jumping from one thing to the next, and never just focusing on one thing until the end of it. Some people are natural multitaskers and can do it fairly well. There are others who cannot multitask because they'll for sure drop the ball somewhere. I'd never say I failed at things because I was a multitasker, but if you had walked into my office to have a conversation with me while I was in the middle of something, I can guarantee you didn't have my full attention. My eyes would be wandering to the computer, checking an email, typing something out as you were talking to me.

Now, imagine your brain is my old office. You're trying to multitask, and you've got your mind on multiple things at once. This makes it hard to keep your focus on one task at a time. This may even cause you to be very forgetful because you're not focused and taking information in like you should be. You're trying to multitask, but you're not focusing on the person who wants—no needs—your attention. Whether that's your husband or significant other, kids, friends, whoever, it can make them feel insignificant to you. As a result, it makes you feel like an awful human being.

If you feel like you have issues focusing your brain or paying attention to others, it's something that's very common with generalized anxiety disorder when our threat indicator is turned up to *high*. You want to pay attention. You don't want to feel like a failure at life, but your brain has a different agenda.

Here are a few ways to help you when you feel like you're struggling to focus.

Eye contact equals (hopefully) a focused mind. When having a conversation with someone, look them right in the eye to increase engagement in conversation. Don't be multitasking, such as folding laundry or doing dishes. (Ironically, I had this thought for the book while I was doing dishes and Billy was talking to me about something that happened at work . . . I swear I'm interested in his job, I really am.)

Make sure others know they have your attention. Give yourself the opportunity to shift your brain's focus to them. In the example of my office, if someone were to walk in while I was in the middle of typing out an email, I could tell them to please sit down and they will have my attention as soon as I've finished. Give yourself the chance to finish the thought, put a period after it, and shift your focus.

Minimize what you've got going on in your life. Lessen the busyness overall. This one is hard, but it will help you with so many other feelings you have regarding your anxiety. Moms are pulled in a million different directions. We have calendars for our calendars for fear we'll forget something. However, the less we have going on, the less we have to think about, right? When we stop multitasking so much in our daily schedules and lives, we can stop feeling like our brain has to multitask as well. I know, this one may not be as doable, but give it a shot if you want.

Make a list and save it for later. Since I'm often forgetful, I love having lists of the things I need to do. So if it can help you, try making a list of the things you have to think about (sounds crazy, I know, but bear with me). Maybe you've got a big decision that's weighing you down and you're worried about it. Maybe you've got a lot going on at work, and it's overwhelming you and making you feel distracted when you're at home. Make a list, put a pin in it, so to speak, and save it to think about later. Of course, make sure you give yourself time later to think about it!

Let others into that brain of yours. Tell someone what you're so worried about and talk it out. Your brain is fixated on it because it thinks whatever you're worried about is a threat. Talking about it with someone else can help you rationalize your brain to no longer be consumed with it.

That last suggestion is so important to me. Whenever I start feeling anxious about something, and I decide to let Billy in on what's going on in my head, I immediately feel better. More often than not, Billy gives me a new perspective, or he offers a solution, or calms my worries in some way. Now, maybe you don't have someone who can support you in the same way, or maybe you don't have a friend or family member you feel like you can confide in. If that's the case, I urge you to find someone. A therapist, a pastor you trust, a total stranger who deals with anxiety as well and can relate (anxiety support groups are a thing)—anyone. Whoever it is, let them in, and let them help you.

Bottom line: Don't let your anxiety weigh down on your relationships or make you feel like a failure. Don't let anxiety affect your mothering, marriage, or friendships. It's your life—not your anxiety's life. So don't let your anxiety and Satan's lies make you feel like you're a failure.

The Stuff to Think About

- When you feel your anxiety rising and you start feeling overwhelmed, what is your common reaction to it? How do you think you can calm yourself and refocus your brain?
- Are there common things that make you feel like a failure when it comes to your anxiety?
- When does your brain typically have a hard time focusing? Is there something that triggers your mind wandering and makes it hard to pay attention? Is there a certain time of the day when it gets worse?

The Stuff to Try Out

- Remind yourself that Satan is the father of lies and give yourself grace when temptation happens. Speak truth to yourself to combat every lie Satan throws at you.
- Try making a list of topics to think about later, and try limiting the load of what you have to think about now by talking to a friend or significant other. Or try limiting your calendar a little bit. Try taking a mommy time-out and researching some breathing techniques as well as some of the other techniques I listed. What's important is not to beat yourself up when your anxiety causes you to be irritable and snappy.

The Truth about It

When he lies, he speaks his native language, for he is a liar and the father of lies. (John 8:44, Jesus speaking of Satan)

But the fruit of the Spirit is love, joy, peace, forbearance, kindness, goodness, faithfulness, gentleness and self-control. (Gal. 5:22–23)

6

The Fear of Attack—a Panic Attack, That Is

(Feeling: I have anxiety about having panic attacks)

I felt really dizzy, like my head was spinning.

I felt as if I was about to throw up. *No, I need to throw up. That would make me feel better*, I thought.

My heart started racing as I felt so nauseated, and I was unable to stand up. I found myself curled up on the floor of the bathroom with my knees in my arms, cradling myself in an attempt to stop the spinning of the room.

"I'm fine," I told Billy. "I just feel nauseated."

He knew; he always knows. I was under stress. I was venturing out of the house during a pandemic for the first time in over a year, and I wasn't feeling great about it.

"Are you sure you're not having a panic attack because you're nervous about tomorrow?" he asked.

"Yeah," I said as the tears started to well up in my eyes. "You know me so well."

It wasn't like it was just any ol' trip out of the house either. I was headed to the dentist. To me, that meant no mask on my face and someone's hands *inside* my mouth. The very thought of it made me want to puke. I had done such a good job of being secluded from the rest of the world in order to keep myself safe, but now I was headed to the dentist because (of course) I thought I had a cavity. There was no escaping it (and normally we escape the dentist for other reasons besides a fear of germs).

Looking back now, it seems silly that I got myself so worked up over something as simple as a dentist appointment, but at that moment, it was a big deal to me. It felt like a life-or-death situation I was facing.

So the next morning, I headed to the dentist with my mask on, my gloves on, and my big girl panties on. I got out of my car and immediately started to feel my anxiety heighten. The thought of interacting with another person besides Billy and the kids made me nervous. *I've totally forgotten how to interact with humans. At least big ones*, I thought.

I walked through the door, breathing heavy through my mask, trying to keep my composure. (Seriously, masks and shortness of breath due to anxiety are not a great mix.) I tried to keep my voice from being shaky as I signed the release form to the best of my ability. I could feel myself on the verge of another panic attack, but I knew I needed to hold it together or there was no way I was going to be able to sit in a chair for thirty minutes while they scraped plaque off my teeth. I made a beeline for the chair so I could calm myself down more as I waited for my turn.

Of course, nothing can get your anxiety going like waiting alone and having nothing else to do but think. As I sat there, tears started to form in my eyes. My anxiety was getting the best of me, and I was imagining myself having a panic attack right there in the waiting room, not sure of how I would explain this to the dental hygienist when she called my name. At this point, I was having anxiety about having a panic attack, not the actual fear of someone else's face all up in my mouth.

And then, I looked up.

The television had HGTV on (as most waiting rooms always do), which held my attention for a moment, but then my eyes wandered just below that. There was a fireplace in the waiting room, and on top of the mantel was a piece of art. Nothing else was sitting on the mantel—no other artwork or knickknacks—just this one picture.

And that picture was of Jesus Christ.

Yup, that's right. Jesus met me in the waiting room while I was on the verge of a panic attack, and seeing His face calmed me down. I mean out of all the things that could have been on the mantel or in the waiting room, there's Jesus! I don't believe it was by accident or chance. (That picture hasn't been there since. I look for it every time I go to the dentist now. I swear I didn't imagine it.) A picture of Jesus is definitely not something you see every day in a waiting room, although it should be! It was a clear sign to me saying, *Courtney, I'm right here with you.* And it was exactly what I needed. My eyes started to tear up again, but this time it was tears of joy.

I knew He was watching over me. I knew I was not facing this fear alone. My breathing returned to normal, so when the hygienist called my name, I smiled, stood up, and walked back with her to get my teeth cleaned. She directed me to the chair and the area I could place my belongings.

"You can go ahead and take your mask off," she said to me.

"Okay, sorry. I'm not used to this at all," I responded.

"Oh, I know! It's so weird not to wear them now!"

"Yeah, um, not so much for me. This is my first big venture out into public," I said. "So . . . I'm not really used to wearing masks at all."

"First big outing and you chose the dentist?" she said with a chuckle. "Well, congratulations, and good for you!"

I smiled and thought, *Yeah, good for me.*

(And no, I didn't have a cavity.)

Panic Attack versus Anxiety Attack: What's the Difference?

In Luke 22:39–46, we see Jesus in the garden of Gethsemane the night He was betrayed, praying to God. He knew what He was about to face. He knew His future was the cross, but He made one last plea to God about whether there might be another way. He was still submitting Himself to God's will. It's not like He was saying, "Yeah, I don't want to do this now." He was more like, "I'll do this, of course, but I'm just wondering if maybe there's another way?" He was experiencing the very human emotion you and I would have experienced: fear.

In verse 44, we read more about Jesus's agony: "And being in anguish, he prayed more earnestly, and his sweat was like drops of blood falling to the ground." Here's a fun fact: Sweating blood is actually a thing our bodies are capable of. It's called hematidrosis, and it is very rare. So rare that doctors don't know what exactly triggers it, but they think it's related to our bodies' fight-or-flight response.[1]

Now, I don't know if Jesus for sure experienced hematidrosis because it's written His sweat was "*like* drops of blood." The other three Gospels don't mention bloody sweat, only Luke's. In Matthew's account of Jesus praying in the garden, Jesus tells His disciples as He's about to pray, "My soul is overwhelmed with sorrow to the point of death. Stay here and keep watch with me" (Matt. 26:38). Bloody sweat or not, Jesus was still overcome with fear and torment.

So if you're tracking with me, this means Jesus—fully God and *still* fully man—had the same emotions and physical effects of anxiety that you and I go through. Panic. Fear. Sweaty agony. Just like you and me. Jesus was still capable of having a very human reaction to fear and distress. And even though He knew the plans God had laid out, He still experienced fear.

Does that give you some comfort for your anxiety? Jesus *knows* what you're feeling when you're stressed or anxious. He *knows* exactly what it's like, having been through it Himself. When you're curled up on the floor in the midst of a panic attack, He doesn't look down at you and say, "Girl, get up, and get over it. Please trust Me more."

No, He's with you in the moment, feeling what you're feeling.

I'm going to say pretty confidently that you've never experienced hematidrosis since it's so rare. But I'm going to bet, since you have anxiety, you have had either a panic attack or an anxiety attack at some point in your life. Everyone's symptoms look different for both, but there is a difference between the two. I used to use these terms interchangeably, but let's take a look at what the difference is. (And you can experience an anxiety attack and a panic attack at the same time . . . because of course you can.)

Panic attacks can occur completely out of the blue. There can be absolutely no reason for them whatsoever. However, they can also be caused by other factors, such as phobias or various triggers. An anxiety attack is typically related to something that's causing you to be stressed or feel threatened, and it can build up gradually because you're obsessing over it and thinking about the threat so much. Panic attacks usually have more intense symptoms and can be debilitating. The reason for this is your autonomous fight-or-flight response is triggered. Anxiety attacks, on the other hand, can be mild, but they can also be more severe. Panic attacks can cause more anxiety over having another panic attack (of course), and having more than one panic attack may be a sign of a panic disorder.[2]

For me, when I'm having a panic attack, I feel sweaty; I'm dizzy, or the room feels like it's spinning; I feel like I need to throw up, or my tummy hurts; my heart is pounding, and my chest hurts; I feel like I'm having a hard time breathing; and I feel out of control. Some people even get shaky or have tingly or numb hands.[3]

When I'm having an anxiety attack, I have a feeling of impending danger or doom, I can feel my heart beating fast in my chest, I'm light-headed, I'm breathing more heavily, I get sweaty, I have gastrointestinal issues (again, sorry if that's TMI for you), and I'm irritable (more than usual). Again, some people may even get shaky or have tingly hands, as with a panic attack.[4]

When you're in the middle of a panic or anxiety attack, it takes over your whole body and makes it hard to function, more so if it's a panic attack. You're not able to think straight, let alone say a prayer asking Jesus to come help a girl out.

The good news is even if you're unable to get that prayer out, Jesus is already on it. He's already there and waiting to help.

He's Gonna Pray for You

I've already mentioned how the Holy Spirit is not one of fear and how God's peace transcends all understanding, but we're going to dive a little deeper with a lesson on the Spirit. If you've been a believer for a while, I'm sure you already know this, but I'm going to review it for the mama reading this who is new to her faith. So if you're more seasoned in your faith, just follow along with me here. It's all going to lead to what He does for us during a panic or anxiety attack, I promise. (And who knows, maybe I'll teach you something new too!)

Even before the gift of His Spirit, we know God is omniscient and knows every little thought that has ever entered our pretty heads. Psalm 139 tells us God can "perceive [our] thoughts from afar" (v. 2) and "before a word is on [our] tongue you, Lord, know it completely" (v. 4). Your thoughts—anxious and all that they are—cannot be hidden from Him even if you tried.

Then came the gift of the Holy Spirit and He changed everything even more (and for the better, of course).

After Jesus ascended to heaven, He sent His Spirit to His disciples and those who believe in Him. You were marked in Him with a seal of the Holy Spirit when you decided to believe in Jesus and accepted Him as your Lord and Savior (Eph. 1:13). This means your body is God's temple for His Spirit, and you are never alone. The Holy Spirit isn't a ghost hovering around you and following you all day; no, He is *within* you, which means His power is within you as well. This power can cast out those fears and fill you with His peace.

In John 14:26, Jesus uses the Greek word *paraklétos* as another name for the Holy Spirit. This means "an advocate, intercessor, a consoler, comforter, helper."[5] Comforter, consoler, helper, advocate—all things we need when it comes to our anxiety, am I right? Jesus goes on to say, "Peace I leave with you; my peace I give you. I do not give to you as the world gives. Do not let your hearts be troubled and do not be afraid" (v. 27). The world can't give to us what Jesus can. The Holy Spirit offers a whole different kind of peace—a peace only He is handing out.

The Spirit helps us and works within us in so many ways, but I want to focus on what He does for us when we're dealing with a panic or anxiety attack. He intercedes on our behalf.

> In the same way, the Spirit helps us in our weakness. We do not know what we ought to pray for, but the Spirit himself intercedes for us through wordless groans. And he who searches our hearts knows the mind of the Spirit, because the Spirit intercedes for God's people in accordance with the will of God. (Rom. 8:26–27)

When you're going through a panic or anxiety attack and you can't pray the prayers, the Spirit prays for you! Isn't that awesome and comforting to know?

As we've learned, King David struggled with anxiety and depression. In Psalm 55, he used words such as "my thoughts trouble me and I am distraught," "my heart is in anguish," "terrors of death," "fear and trembling," and "horror has overwhelmed me" (vv. 2–5). I have no idea if he was experiencing a panic attack at this moment (or if he'd ever had a panic attack in his life), but the words "anguish," "terror," and "fear and trembling" sound too familiar to me. Later in verse 22, we read, "Cast your cares on the LORD and he will *sustain* you" (other translations such as the ESV or ERV use words like "cast your burden" or "give your worries"). I added emphasis to this one because David didn't write that he was healed or that his anguish was completely taken from him. Nope, David wrote that God heard his voice, saved him, and *sustained* him.

I can't promise you a panic or anxiety attack will never happen again. I can't promise your panic attacks will get less severe or be shorter (the average panic attack is between five and twenty minutes[6]). What I can promise is that a prayer is being delivered to God and He's hearing it. He hears it, and He will sustain you through whatever suffering you're enduring at that very moment. Through sustenance and prayer, He is strengthening us. Psalm 138:3 says, "As soon as I pray, you answer me; you encourage me by giving me strength" (NLT).

Strength is what you'll for sure get. Strength to fight through that panic attack and come out on the other side of it. Strength to move forward without fear of another attack coming on. Strength to gain control and slow your breathing. Strength to make it through those five, ten, maybe even twenty minutes of your body being consumed with fear. The Holy Spirit is all on it, and He's advocating for you. He'll be right there ready and waiting to be your strength through it all.

The rest may not be known, but mark my words, God is within you, and He'll sustain you.

Yeah, I'm All Panicky about Having Another Panic Attack

"Oh, no! Please, God! Please, God, make it stop. Make it stop!"

I had just rolled over in bed. I *was* asleep and from what I can recall, it was a peaceful sleep undisturbed by kids crying in the night or a snoring husband. But as soon as I had rolled over onto my right side, the room was spinning. It was full-on out of control spinning. Not the dizzy kind of spinning but the *I'm on the teacups at Disney World and the whole world is moving* kind of spinning. Except I wasn't on a spinning teacup. I was sitting up straight in my bed, and the room was still going on the teacup ride. Until—

Oh my gosh, I have to barf.

Billy woke up not knowing what the heck was going on except that his wife was screaming to God then hovered over the toilet throwing up from motion sickness.

"What's going on?"

"I can't make it stop. I can't make the room stop spinning," I cried out in panic.

I'm dying, I thought. *This is what the end looks like for me.*

I had accepted only two options here: either I had some sort of disease, or this was death.

I couldn't get it to stop. It was worse when I'd try to lay back down in bed, so I went to the recliner in the living room to sit myself up. After close to an hour of experiencing this and a phone call to the nurse line at the hospital, I decided to go into the emergency room.

After two hours in the ER, several prayers, blood work, neurological tests, and an IV to keep me hydrated, we came to the conclusion that . . . we didn't know.

Most likely it was caused by ear crystals, the doctor said. We (apparently) have crystals in our ears, and when they become dislodged, they can give you the vertigo feeling. No one could really give me a firm solution or treatment for it besides a prescription-strength version of Dramamine. So I went home and was consumed with fear that I would have another vertigo episode.

The idea of not knowing (for sure) what triggered the vertigo and not having any real solution to put a stop to it got my anxiety up. Questions like, *What if it's brain cancer?* were going through my head. I was afraid to turn over in bed again for fear an ear crystal would set off the dizziness. As a result, I had a few panic attacks about the fear of having vertigo—which caused more dizziness, which caused even more fear that I might have a panic attack.

And I think you know where I'm going with this.

Anxiety about having anxiety. (Remember? I said this was a thing!)

Anxiety about anxiety, or anxiety about having a panic or anxiety attack is something that sounds absurd and probably very dramatic, but it's something I pray about all the time. Which brings us back to our good friend Paul.

In 2 Corinthians 12:7, Paul describes a "thorn in [his] flesh" that was sent to "torment" him. His thorn was not anxiety or a mental illness (I'm assuming), but it still tortured him to the point where he prayed three times that the Lord would take it from him. Paul writes the Lord's response in verses 9–10: "But he said to me, 'My grace is sufficient for you, for *my power is made perfect in weakness.*' Therefore I will boast all the more gladly about my weaknesses, so that *Christ's power may rest on me.* That is why, for Christ's sake, I *delight in weaknesses,* in insults, in hardships, in persecutions, in difficulties. *For when I am weak, then I am strong*" (emphasis added).

God is strong—not this girl.

I am weak so His strength and power can be made perfect.

If you're having anxiety about having anxiety or about having a panic attack, know that His power is made perfect through your weakness. (And it's probably safe to say that having anxiety about panic attacks will *probably* not help keep you from having another panic attack. Just a guess.) When a panic attack hits, just know His strength is being displayed through it all.

Of course, your panic attacks may be a part of a panic disorder, and there is no probable cause or trigger that sets it off. Maybe you haven't been diagnosed with a panic disorder. But if this is at all ringing a bell for you, please call your doctor. When it comes to panic attacks, medication and therapy can help (we'll learn more about this later). And if you struggle finding relief from medical help, just remember God is with you through it all. The Holy Spirit is praying for you on your behalf, and His strength is made perfect through your weakness. And that is why I'm going to delight in my weaknesses. (Can I get an amen?)

Baby Steps

The Stuff to Think About

- Have you ever experienced a panic attack? Or an anxiety attack? If you ever have and never knew there was a difference, consider which of the two you're more prone to have.

- Have you ever considered the fact that Jesus understands your anxiety? Being fully man and fully God, He knows exactly what you're going through and can comfort you more than someone who's never experienced a panic or anxiety attack.

The Stuff to Try Out

- When you're going through a panic attack, always remember the Holy Spirit dwells within you and is praying on your behalf. Jesus knows what you're feeling, and He is with you, feeling it alongside you.

- Having anxiety about having another panic attack is normal, but it's probably going to lead to another anxiety attack. Look at other techniques to help combat your anxiety, such as yoga, meditation, medication, and counseling.

- If you believe you are prone to panic attacks and you think you may have a panic disorder, please talk to your doctor about treatment options.

The Truth about It

In the same way, the Spirit helps us in our weakness. We do not know what we ought to pray for, but the Spirit himself intercedes for us through wordless groans. And he who searches our hearts knows the mind of the Spirit, because the Spirit intercedes for God's people in accordance with the will of God. (Rom. 8:26–27)

But he said to me, "My grace is sufficient for you, for my power is made perfect in weakness." Therefore I will boast all the more gladly about my weaknesses, so that Christ's power may rest on me. That is why, for Christ's sake, I delight in weaknesses, in insults, in hardships, in persecutions, in difficulties. For when I am weak, then I am strong. (2 Cor. 12:9–10)

I've Got a Lot Going On— My Mind Is Racing

(Feeling: I overthink and obsess about everything)

"Why do you always have to obsess about something?"

Billy thought he was being funny as I was telling him about what I had going on in my brain at that moment.

"I don't know. Why don't you talk to my anxiety about it?!" (I can be pretty funny, too, sometimes—or maybe not.)

"I do . . . a lot! I mean, that's who I'm talking to right now," he responded in a matter-of-fact way.

Sound about right?

How many conversations do you have with someone when they're talking to your anxiety and not necessarily to just you? This is pretty much how it goes when you're overthinking or obsessing about something. Your anxiety kicks in and says, "Hey, think about this and how big of a threat it is. Why don't you go over all of the what-if scenarios and play it out in your brain for a few hours? Maybe even a few days?"

Yeah.

My counselor actually once asked me what I do when my anxiety starts to tell me there's a threat. You want to know what I told her?

"I talk back to my anxiety."

You may be thinking, *Okay, Courtney, that sounds like something a crazy person would do! I'm not going to do that.* Sounds crazy, I know. I'm over here having conversations with myself in my head. But it's truly something that can help when you feel your mind spiraling, and it's a trick I got from *The Unraveling Podcast* with Kelli Bachara.[1] (She's also a mental health therapist, so she knows what she's talking about.)

Here's an example of what a conversation with my anxiety might sound like.

Anxiety: "Hey, I know you're trying to sleep, but you should really be worried about that conversation you have to have tomorrow with so-and-so. Why don't we sit here and play the conversation over in our head until one o'clock in the morning? Sound good?"

Me: "Yeah, no. God tells me not to worry about tomorrow. So I think I'm going to sleep instead. Plus, I know that conversation may not go like how I play it out in my mind, and I would've wasted precious sleep time worrying about it."

Anxiety: "Do you want to think about your next five-year plan? Let's think about your career plans when the kids are in school, or maybe what you want to do with your life."

Me: "Nah, God's got a plan for me, and I know it's all good. He'll steer me in the right direction when it's time."

Anxiety: "Okay, well, how about the incident that happened today with William? That's not worrying about tomorrow; that happened today. Let's think about that."

Me: "... I don't want to."

Anxiety: "Sure you do. You're worried about what his behavior says about you as a mom. You're worried about

him going to school and behaving like that with his
teacher. You're worried if you handled it the correct
way or if you've ruined him for life."

Me: "Gosh, what if he does that in front of the whole class?
What does that say about me as a mom? Ugh. No!
Not doing this! I'm not a perfect mom, but I'm a good
one. William is a good boy, and he will be just fine. I'm
going to sleep now."

Anxiety: "Okay, well, I'll be here in the morning."

Me: "Oh, yeah. I know you will."

Okay, maybe that's not always how it goes. I'm sure I get off
course and go down the rabbit hole more times than I can count,
but you get the idea. It's one tactic that may help you control your
thought pattern and move on to another one.

Sometimes when we get to overthinking and obsessing, it's like
a pinball machine. Your anxiety has hit the Ball Launch button, and
the ball has been shot up into the playfield. You don't have control
over the game; your anxiety is the one with its hands on the Flipper buttons. (Yes, I researched pinball terminology, okay? I'm not
making this stuff up!) Your anxiety is controlling the game, and
the ball is bouncing from one thought to the next. That flipper (or
your anxiety) is shooting it back up any time the ball is close to
falling down the out hole. And you're just sitting there praying for
the game to be over.

Another way to think of it is that it's kind of like you've got a song
on repeat in your brain. It's like that old CD player where the song is
skipping and keeps repeating itself. Or you've set the song on repeat
because it's your favorite jam. Even when the song has finished, it can
still be stuck in your brain for hours later. Whether your thoughts are
something your anxiety perceives as a threat or they're something
you're obsessing about, it's annoyingly hard to turn them off.

Oh, but wait! There are more mind tricks your anxiety can
play on you. Another thing that can be common with anxiety are

intrusive thoughts. Let me give you an example of a recurring intrusive thought I have. I have a catwalk in my house that looks down into my living room and connects the kids' two rooms. Several times, I have walked across it while holding a child, and an image of me tripping and dropping my kid over the railing will come to my mind. (I know, pretty terrible.) Sometimes while I'm driving, images will pop into my head of being in a car wreck and turning behind me to see one child knocked out in the wreckage and the other child crying. I'll be honest; I've had even more disturbing thoughts than that enter my mind.

You can call it Satan.

You can call it an intrusive thought.

It could be a combo of both, depending on how much you let the thought win. Either way, I think we can agree they're unwanted thoughts, and some of them are downright disturbing. Everyone may occasionally experience intrusive thoughts; however, when those intrusive thoughts become more common for you and disrupt your daily life, that's when they may be a symptom of anxiety, depression, obsessive-compulsive disorder (OCD), or PTSD.[2]

Intrusive thoughts can appear out of nowhere and usually, because of their nature, can cause a lot of anxiety. I know I will sit there and obsess over what my thought means, like is it my mind's way of trying to tell me something? Or I'll sit there and beat myself up for thinking something so disturbing, and I'll analyze what kind of a person I am. But here's something I constantly have to remind myself: they're just thoughts. The brain is complex and fun sometimes, but intrusive thoughts don't mean squat.

What's important is not to let the intrusive thought take over. Don't sit there and fixate on it. Don't even sit there and keep playing out the scenario; you don't need to see how the end of the skit will play out. Don't sit there and freak out about how awful it is or could be. There's nothing wrong with you, so don't panic. The thought does not need to take over and consume you for the next eight to ten hours of the day. It's just an unwanted thought. Remind yourself of a Bible verse that points you to the truth versus the intrusive thought flashing through your mind, then move on. When you let the thought take control, Satan wins. The thought may be a normal part of human life, but letting the thought consume you, that's exactly what he wants.

To further prove my point, let's look at a verse from Proverbs. Proverbs 4:23 says, "Above all else, guard your heart, for everything you do flows from it." You may think this is a weird verse to look at in a book about anxiety, but let me go on. The word "heart" is not just referring to your pumping blood organ located in your chest. In biblical Hebrew, there wasn't a word for "mind." The heart was the center of a person's mind and soul; therefore, the word *lēḇ* in Hebrew means "heart" as we know it, but it was also used to refer to the inner man, mind, and understanding.[3] Other translations of this verse use the words "guard your thoughts" (CEV), "protect your mind" (CEB), or "be careful what you think" (ERV).

Guard your *mind*, for everything you do flows from it.

Your joy flows from it. That loving and kind heart of yours flows from it. Your peace flows from it. Your gratitude flows from it.

Your anxiety may be a persistent presence in your mind, but it does not need to be in control of you. Quit bouncing the pinball, move on to the next song, guard your mind, take back control, and . . .

Game over.

The Girl Who Cried "Labor"

"It looks like you are three centimeters dilated and, uh, about 70 percent effaced already," the doctor told me as he was finishing up my exam.

"Are you kidding me?" I tried to sound composed while trying not to freak out.

"Yeah, if I had to guess, I'm going to say you'll deliver within the next week or two."

No, please, God, this isn't happening. That's way too early.

"Should I go on bed rest or something? What can we do to keep her in there longer?" I asked, trying to hold back the tears. "My sister was given a shot to stop her labor with her second kid; can we do that?"

"Anything after thirty-four weeks we don't try to stop or prolong labor. You could go longer, but we just have to leave it up to your body at this point. And baby."

I was thirty-four weeks pregnant with Adelyn, and after the premature birth of William (I'm sure you recall that story from chapter 3), I was nervous. Scratch that—I had been living one anxiety attack after another for eight months, and this was just the icing on top of the cake.

The anxiety started with a subchorionic hemorrhage when I was twelve weeks pregnant with Adelyn. Basically, I was hemorrhaging between the placenta and the uterine wall. I bled off and on for the first month of my pregnancy, living in constant fear the placenta would completely detach and I would miscarry. Then I went from that to week sixteen through thirty-six where I was getting jabbed with a needle every week at the doctor's office. I was receiving progesterone shots to try to stop my water from spontaneously breaking like it did with William.

So when I began having Braxton Hicks contractions at thirty weeks, I knew it was false labor. Then the contractions began to get more . . . real. And that brings us to this thirty-four-week checkup where I was being told I'd probably deliver within a week or two. Glad I could catch you up.

Let's put it this way: You don't tell a preemie mama who suffers from an anxiety disorder that she may very well be having another preemie baby. She immediately starts overthinking, and her imagination starts pointing to all the NICU nightmare scenarios. And when her mind begins to wander, she starts to believe it's all coming to fruition.

"Babe, I'm heading to Target. I'm going to go get a blood pressure cuff. I think my blood pressure is high. My heart is pounding so hard in my chest." (In my defense, you may remember that I had preeclampsia with William, so this wasn't a totally off-the-wall, irrational fear.)

It was Christmas Eve, and I had woken up in a panic thinking my blood pressure was high. I could hear my heart beating through my chest, and my mind immediately began to think there was a problem. In all honesty, it was probably my anxiety. Who am I kidding? It totally was my anxiety, but it had me believing something was off and I needed to take my blood pressure ASAP.

Fwoosh.

The reading was like 140/90, so not super high, but high enough to call the nurse. We headed to the hospital, thinking we'd have a Christmas baby. *That would be pretty cool*, I thought. *She'd share a birthday with Jesus.*

Nope, she wouldn't. Apparently, the blood pressure cuff needed to be calibrated.

So one week later . . .

"Honey, I've been having contractions again, and I don't think they're Braxton Hicks this time. They're coming pretty regularly and not going away when I change positions. I think this might be it!"

Technically, I was induced with William, so I had no clue what was supposed to happen if I were to go into labor on my own. I was obsessing and convinced the contractions this time were real. My mind could not convince me otherwise. So I spent New Year's Eve in triage. (If you're tracking with me, yes, I spent Christmas Eve and New Year's Eve in triage. Apparently, I really wanted a baby born on a holiday . . . plus a tax credit.)

But nope, it wasn't time yet. It turned out I was dehydrated, which induced the contractions, but they were false labor contractions.

However, according to the triage doctor, it only takes two high blood pressure readings while you're pregnant to be diagnosed with gestational hypertension. And you guessed it, my blood pressure was high when I got to triage—but just twice. They kept me overnight for observation. My blood pressure remained completely normal throughout the night; it was only those two first readings that were high. However, it was decided a couple days later to go ahead and induce me. They were certain, even though my blood pressure had gone back down, it was a sign I was developing pre-eclampsia again, and they wanted to get Adelyn out.

I'm not an obstetrician, but when a mama goes into triage, she's probably anxious to some degree. She doesn't need to have an anxiety disorder for that to be a fact. But since I *am* a mama with anxiety, I think it's safe to assume my anxiety was to blame for those two high blood pressure readings. My medical records may be labeled as gestational hypertension, but I'm pretty sure Adelyn was born when she was because of my anxiety. I actually researched this, and anxiety can cause your blood pressure to rise temporarily.[4] So there you go.

And boy was I relieved to get her out. *Yes, please just get her out already and end this insanity*, I thought. I wanted to put an end to the trips to triage and all the obsessing about it. I wanted the anxiety and the overthinking to stop. I was tired of worrying any time something felt off or my imagination convinced me something was off. I was also tired of looking like an idiot to my family as I kept telling them, "I think today is the day!" I was a nervous wreck.

A little over eleven hours of labor and a few good pushes, and Adelyn was here.

I had made it to thirty-seven weeks.

What Are You So Worried About?

I'm about to get real with you here, and I'd appreciate no judgment. I know I've been very real and open until this point, but this next section is going to be even more vulnerable. So please, remember I'm human, I have anxiety, God loves me, and He says you should love me too; got it? Okay, here it comes.

I'm calling it "Confessions of an Obsessive Mom," and it's all the things I obsess about.

My feet. Maybe this should be named as a phobia, but I don't like other people's feet. On top of that, I'm obsessed with my own feet being clean before going to bed. I've tried working through this one, but I will literally lay there in bed fixating on the feeling of my dirty feet in between the sheets. However, when Jesus washed His disciples' feet at the Last Supper, Peter asked that not only his feet be cleaned but his hands and head as well. Jesus responded and said if the feet are clean, the whole body is clean (John 13:10). So any time Billy teases me about my clean feet thing, I point him to Scripture. Yes, I know that's not literally what Jesus is talking about, but I'm not ready to give up my feet thing. And no, I wash more than just my feet before bed. But definitely my feet. (Yes, it's weird, I know.)

My nightly routine. I call it a security check, but basically I check the doors, the burners (thanks to the neighbor's house fire in chapter 1), and the security system to make sure it is armed. I do this three times—safety first?

Conversations with others. It's like a dialogue in my head, like I'm an author of a script and I'm playing it out with others. It's useful when I have a difficult conversation coming up with someone who may be confrontational (like from my former HR days). However, it's annoying when it's a stupid little thing that becomes a full-on skit in my mind. I'm sure this is normal. Right? I'm not alone, am I?

The future. I used to have a five-year plan all mapped out. I planned out babies (to the day, or at least I tried to), and my career was all planned out with promotions and all. Every little life decision was laid out in five-year increments. This isn't a big thing for me anymore since I became a stay-at-home mom. I've put the future in God's hands. Took me years to do it, but I'm leaving it with Him.

My health. Just this past year, my doctor ordered a mammogram for me (to be fair, my mother had breast cancer), I've done physical therapy for what I thought was a pinched nerve, I've gone to the ER with vertigo thinking I was dying, I've been to a neurologist to discuss numbness in my arms, and I've had an MRI done on my brain.

(Yeah, my deductible will be met soon.) I trust God will bring me to heaven whenever the date is set, but I still can't help but obsess over all the little things that go on in my body. Most of the time, ironically, I find it's something caused by my anxiety (for instance, the gastroenterologist experience I've already shared with you). Anxiety does weird things to your body, and my imagination can't help it. Plus, I like answers. Maybe it's a little bit of hypochondria. Trust me, I'm working on this one.

Some of these confessions may sound very OCD to you. To be honest, it's probably because they are. I've never been diagnosed with OCD, but maybe I should be. OCD and anxiety are two distinct mental health conditions; however, they do share some similarities, and a person can have them both at the same time.[5]

If our brain senses a threat, it will obsess about that threat and how best to avoid it. When we take action to avoid it over and over again, it's more than just a habit and it *can* become an OCD compulsion. (For example, my fear of germs during the pandemic led me to compulsively sanitize everything and wash my hands till they bled.) So which comes first—the anxiety or the OCD? Depends on what happened first. Is it a compulsion based on a threat our anxiety has convinced us about, or is it a compulsion we feel like we have to do that's causing us to be anxious if we don't get to do it?

I don't know where you're at in your faith journey, but chances are if you've been a Christian for a long time and had anxiety for a while, you've probably read Luke 12:22–34. It's titled "Do Not Worry." Basically, it's Jesus preaching and telling us, well, don't worry about it. Jesus points out the birds do not need to worry about where they'll get their food because God provides for them. He also says the flowers do not worry about what they look like because God will make them beautiful. Jesus gives these examples because *God loves you more* than the birds and the flowers. If He provides and cares for them, He surely will provide and take care of you. Jesus offers a complete mic drop verse, "Who of you by worrying can add a single hour to your life?" (v. 25).

Tomorrow is not guaranteed. God has already numbered your days, so worrying about it doesn't change the outcome. But I know your worries seem way bigger in your mind. I know your mind can take those worries and string them out for days. I know your mind will play out every scenario and make you feel like a toddler for how wild your imagination can get. I know your mind is up against you, my friend. Jesus tells you not to worry, but your body tells you you've got something to worry about. (And who knows, maybe you really do. I don't know your current circumstances, but you could be going through something scary and worrisome. Jesus gets that.)

So I've come up with a little acronym for you. This isn't something that's been scientifically proven since, you know, I'm not the expert. And it may not even be super useful to you, but it's how I deal with worry. Are you ready for it? The acronym is WORRY. (Pretty clever, huh?)

W—*Word of God.* Your first defense is God and what He has to say about whatever it is you're worrying about. He speaks to you through Scripture, and He is best at calming your worries.

O—*Observe.* Observe the thought or the worry. Is it rational? Is it something within your control? Is it stealing your joy or your sleep away from you? Should it be having this much control over you?

R—*Retreat and run away from it.* Guard your mind and get far away from the worrisome thoughts. Turn your mind to something else completely.

R—*Request (but really you're going to pray about it).* Request God to take the worry from you, and pray He calms your anxious heart.

Y—*You're not alone.* This is one thing I'll preach about a lot in this book because anxiety will lie to you and tell you

you're crazy and the only one like this. *You're not alone.* You're not the only worrywart in the world. There are a ton of worrisome mamas out there, more than you could even imagine (sadly so). Take comfort in the fact that you're not the only one *and* you have God with you throughout it all.

And I'm not saying you need to WORRY in this order. Prayer is probably first, or maybe you'd want to do it last. It doesn't matter. These are just some steps you can take when the worry starts to flood you, and I'm hoping they help.

Let's talk about another thing you've probably felt before when it came to your anxiety—indecisiveness. Am I right? I'm betting you have struggled with this.

You may have been told you're just an indecisive person, but I suspect that your indecisiveness is related to your anxiety. Since you may like to play out all the what-if scenarios when it comes to decisions, your anxiety doesn't know which scenarios look most appealing. It may be blatantly obvious or maybe not. Let's take a look at a scenario I've played out recently, and we'll read it as a conversation between my anxiety and me again (because that was fun).

Me: "I don't know which schooling option to pick for William. There are so many options these days, and it's not like it was when I was a kid. There are public schools, private schools, Christian schools, Montessori schools, charter schools, homeschool, aaah! Too many options!"

Anxiety: "Why don't you homeschool him so he never leaves the house and you never have to take your eyes off of him? You can control him forever!"

Me: "Yeah, but then he'll lack socialization skills. Plus, math scares me."

Anxiety: "Schools are scary these days. It's not like when you were a kid. With all the school shootings there have been lately your child will have to go through metal detectors just to get inside of the classroom and remove his backpack for it to be searched. You don't want your child living with that fear every day."

Me: "Ugh! I'm done with this conversation! I'll just make this decision another day. Or I'll tell Billy to make it for me."

See! Indecisive.

Here's my advice for when you're having a hard time making a decision and your anxiety is making it impossible for you to decide. Look at the WORRY acronym again. Talk to God about it in prayer. Look at what God says about it in the Bible. Talk about it with someone because you're not alone. More than likely someone else has had to make this decision before. Decide if it's really a life-or-death decision and whether it deserves you obsessing over it. Then run away from it. Make the decision and don't look back. Stand firm in the choice you've made and move on.

When in doubt, trust your mom gut because it's probably listening to the Holy Spirit versus anxiety.

The Stuff to Think About

- Have you ever experienced an intrusive thought? Did you obsess over it, or were you able to move on pretty quickly? (I'm assuming you obsessed because your anxiety told you to, but who knows?)
- Do you believe you have some OCD compulsions as well? Do you constantly find yourself doing some of the same

things over and over again? If you've never been diagnosed with OCD, consider talking to your doctor if you believe you might have both.

- If you're an indecisive person like me, have you ever considered that your anxiety is to blame? What types of things do you tend to struggle with when making decisions? Little things like what to make for dinner? Or are you up all night worrying about school options and whether to vaccinate your kids?

The Stuff to Try Out

- Try talking back to your anxiety when it starts to tell you to worry. Speak truth to it—that God tells you not to worry—and shut it down.
- When you feel your mind starting to bounce around and become filled with worry, use the WORRY acronym to combat it. Shut down the worry—game over.
- When intrusive thoughts start to pop into your mind, combat them with biblical truth, and don't let the thoughts have control over you.
- When it comes to being indecisive due to your worrying brain, listen to the Spirit, trust your mom gut, make the choice, and stand firm in it.

The Truth about It

> Above all else, guard your heart,
> for everything you do flows from it. (Prov. 4:23)

Who of you by worrying can add a single hour to your life? (Luke 12:25)

Sorry, Kids—Mommy's Too Tired Today

(Feeling: I can't turn my brain off to sleep and I'm so exhausted)

Creak. Thump.

I turned to look at my phone, and it was 2:00 a.m. I could hear footsteps walking toward my bedroom. Billy was traveling for work and it was my first time alone in the new house with baby William. I peeked over at him in his bassinet; he was sound asleep. The footsteps kept making their way to our room. I didn't have anything near me to defend myself. All the knives were in the kitchen, the baseball bat in the garage. The keys to the car were out of my reach; they were in the mudroom, and the nearest exit out of my house was a window. I didn't have shoes. There wasn't time to even put socks on. I quickly snatched my baby out of his bassinet and slid open the nearest window. The darn thing wouldn't open! I struggled to get it and eventually pushed with all my might and shoved the screen out. I escaped, running barefoot across the yard to the nearest neighbor's house . . .

Nope, didn't happen. Just a scenario played out in my mind, multiple times, if I'm being honest.

But I remember the first time being home alone with my baby at night while Billy was gone for work, and it was miserable. I wanted to move the dresser in front of the bedroom door. I had been alone before while Billy traveled for work. I never thought of myself as someone who was reliant on a man to make her feel safe. However, everything changed when I became a mom and had a helpless, sleeping baby lying next to me. I was all alone. I just laid there awake all night long, listening to the noises of the house.

The *creak* of the house settling.

The *thump* of the heater turning on.

The *pitter patter* of the mice above my head. (Yes, it grosses me out too, but I'm giving you an accurate picture of my life.)

I'd love to say this was the only time I've laid awake all night long, watching the hours on the clock pass, listening to my noisy house—but it's not. Even when Billy is home, sleeping right next to me, I can do this. Even in the days before motherhood, I could let my brain spiral from one thought to the next. Even after we installed a security system, I could still lie there and play out scenarios in my mind of intruders in the house and how I would get to my sleeping kids in their rooms and escape.

All. Night. Long.

I don't want to be in my thirties and scared of all the things that go bump in the night. I don't want a simple little noise to cause my imagination to run away from me and play out terrifying scenarios.

Psalm 121 comforts me, and I want to leave it right here for you. If you can relate to any of this or not, I think it'll bring you some comfort.

> I lift up my eyes to the mountains—
>   where does my help come from?
> My help comes from the LORD,
>   the Maker of heaven and earth.

He will not let your foot slip—
    he who watches over you will not slumber;
indeed, he who watches over Israel
    will neither slumber nor sleep.

The LORD watches over you—
    the LORD is your shade at your right hand;
the sun will not harm you by day,
    nor the moon by night.

The LORD will keep you from all harm—
    he will watch over your life;
the LORD will watch over your coming and going
    both now and forevermore.

While there is a lot of comfort to be found in this psalm, here's the biggest comfort as it relates to this chapter: God doesn't sleep. He doesn't have to. He watches over you and your babies. All night, every night. He's got His eyes on it all so you can shut yours and get some rest. When things go bump in the night, remind yourself of that truth. It's just a noise. He's watching over you and your kids.

And if there's a really loud noise or something of concern, well, I usually nudge Billy and wake him up to go investigate. He loves having a jumpy, frightened wife who wakes him up over random noises every night.

Moms Don't Sleep. Period.

Trying to sleep with anxiety is already fun enough as it is, but then when you add in the job of motherhood and how we're on call 24/7, it makes sleep even more impossible. Without fail, as soon as you've drifted off to sleep and are deep into your REM cycle, something or someone wakes you up. And then there's my favorite nightly interruption since becoming a mother—having to pee. Either way, no matter what it is that wakes you up, when you're awake, you're awake. And once you're good and awake, your mind starts racing.

Nighttime is when my anxiety gets set to high gear because it's when my brain has the most time to think. It sucks. I don't want to sit up all night thinking about . . . I don't even know if I could tell you what I'm thinking about! That's how useless and a waste of time it is for me!

I've sat there thinking about something for what seems like forever, drifted off to sleep, and then woke up a few hours later and my mind picked back up right where it left off. (Please tell me I'm not the only one this has happened to.) My mind will carry on with the worry and reengage like it never went to sleep. Pretty crazy, huh? Well, not totally crazy. Our minds never truly rest. Even when you're sleeping, you're still dreaming away.

They. Don't. Turn. Off.

So what do I do when my mind starts going at night? Couple of things.

Going back to my little WORRY acronym, I retreat from the thoughts. I'm not sure if there's a clinical term for this or not, but I go to my happy place. Really, I could just focus on a happy thought from the day or turn my mind in a different direction entirely, but I like to shut down the anxiety pinball machine by visiting one of my favorite places in the world.

In my happy place, I'm a kid at my grandparents' house. I imagine Nana standing at the kitchen counter, making me French toast or slurping a chocolate malt through a straw as we have a little treat in the afternoon. I imagine Papa sitting at the kitchen table with a plate of bacon and a cup of coffee in front of him while he reads the newspaper. It's a happy memory from my childhood, and it's a peaceful place in my mind. There are no worrisome thoughts there. There are no scary memories filled with fear. It's just calm and safe. And eventually, after spending time in my happy place, my mind eventually drifts off to sleep with the rest of me. The spinning thoughts are halted with a pin put in them for another day.

Another tactic I use at night is talking to God. Of course, sometimes this doesn't result in me going back to sleep very quickly because by now you may have noticed I like to talk. (In this case, I'm writing to you, but you're getting a good taste of my personality. I'm a rambler, I know.) Some nights I can get going for quite a while with God and talk His ear off. But I feel it's a more productive use of my time. Instead of sitting there and focusing on the things worrying me, I'm taking them to God and talking to Him about the worry. Usually, it goes something like this:

Hey, God, it's me again. You know what I'm worried about? I'm really worried about my kids and this world we live in right now. Bullies, YouTube, ya know, that kind of stuff. I really want to lock them up in this house for another fifteen to seventeen years until I'm unable to legally do so. It's hard because I worry about them when I don't have my eyes on them. You may not get that because Your eyes are on everything all the time, but You know what I mean. I just get so worried all of the time. I'm so afraid I'm going to mess up. I know I only have a set number of years with them here in my home, and I don't want to screw it up. I want to raise them to love You and love others. God, I pray they grow up to love You. I pray I'm pointing them in the right direction.

And then I fall asleep.

God is probably tired of the rambling, and He puts me to sleep so He doesn't have to hear it anymore. (I'm totally kidding. I don't think that's how He operates.) I used to feel guilty about falling asleep while talking to God. I used to think I was an awful Christian for sleeping in the middle of a prayer. However, I saw a social media post a year or so ago and it kind of put it into perspective for me.

Imagine your child has woken up in the middle of the night with a bad dream. He or she has called out to Mommy to come and comfort them. Maybe your child is really little, and you decide to rock them back to sleep. Maybe they're older and too big for your arms, so you lie in bed with them and hold them in your arms until they drift off. Either way, your presence has comforted them. Your being there has made them feel safe and has given them peace. I imagine the same is true for God and me, or God and you.

Let's put it this way. If your kid has a bad dream or they get hurt with a boo-boo, who do they run to?

Mama.

If they're scared for any reason or worried about something, who do they go to?

Mama. (And maybe Dad too. I'm not discounting Daddy's role here, okay?)

My point is, you are your children's safe haven and their greatest comforter—and God is your greatest comforter. Isaiah 66:13 tells us God will comfort us just as a mother comforts her child. Remember, we're seeking comfort for our anxiety so we can take our joy back.

So when a scary noise wakes me up in the night, He's there to comfort me and reassure me everything is okay.

When I wake up to pee and worries come to mind, He's there to put my mind at rest.

When I have a hard time turning my brain off, He's there putting me back to sleep.

Plain and simple. If I fall asleep talking to God, it's because He's rocked me back to sleep. He's cradling me in His arms as I'm spooked about a noise I heard or getting long-winded about all the worries of the world. I picture Him saying, "Time to go to sleep, Courtney. You're safe, My daughter. I'm right here."

Maybe you've never fallen asleep talking to God. Maybe you're too good and awake when your mind gets going. Maybe the thing your mind is fixated on and has you worried about is something you *need* to take to God to talk it out with Him. Maybe you're in need of His advice and you've had no time in your busy day to talk to Him and sort it out. Psalm 16:7 reads, "I will bless the Lord who counsels me—even at night when my thoughts trouble me" (CSB).

We've established God is up all night long, but have you ever thought about how His presence might be felt most at night? Have you ever thought God speaks to you more clearly at night? When the house is quiet and there are no kids interrupting your thoughts, maybe that's just the time of day to get your moment with God. Maybe that's the time where He counsels you the most because you can hear Him more clearly without all the other noise going on around you.

In the very beginning of 1 Samuel, we see a young woman named Hannah praying for a son after years of infertility. She prayed that if God answered her prayer, she would dedicate her child to serve the Lord. She then gave birth to Samuel, and after Samuel had been weaned, she upheld her promise and sent him to serve at the house of the Lord with a priest named Eli. In chapter 3, we see Samuel being woken up in the night to the sound of his name being called. Three times, he goes to Eli and says, "Here I am; you called me" (v. 5). After the third time, Eli realized it was God trying to talk to Samuel. Samuel had never heard God's voice before and was totally unaware. Eli told him, "Go and lie down, and if he calls you, say, 'Speak, Lord, for your servant is listening'" (v. 9). And that's exactly what Samuel did the next time God called his name.

Speak, Lord, for Your servant is listening.

You may have noticed in my ramblings to God, I did all the talking. There wasn't much space for a breath between my thoughts, or in this case, a period. I was going and going, letting my mind race. I imagine when I would start getting long-winded, God was probably like, "Courtney, can you let Me do some of the talking for once?" It's something I'm working on, for sure. But if I can silence the noise going on in my head at night, if I can quiet my thoughts long enough to listen to God, I may receive better counsel for all my worries. Instead of just casting my anxiety on Him, I may actually receive answers to my worries. I may receive direction to all the decisions I'm obsessing about.

Samuel wasn't the only one who received visits from God at night. We see God speak to Isaac at night and tell him that He will bless him and increase the number of his descendants (Gen. 26:24).

We see Jacob wrestling at night with God until daybreak (Gen. 32:22–32). We see God appear to Solomon at night as Solomon asks for wisdom and knowledge (2 Chron. 1:7–10). We see Daniel receive a vision at night concerning the mystery of King Nebuchadnezzar's dream (Dan. 2:19). We see Paul receive a vision at night from the Lord, encouraging him not to be afraid and not to stay silent (Acts 18:9).

I'm not saying every time you're unable to sleep, lie there awake for a good five hours and wait for God to talk to you. I know you need your beauty sleep; we all do. But my point is, if you're lying awake at night and unable to sleep because of what's going on in your brain, it's more productive to talk to God about it rather than sit there and have your wheels spin all night on the same thought. Maybe you're awake thinking about it for a reason, and the reason is God wants to tell you something.

The very idea for this book came to me in the middle of the night after having a panic attack. I'm sure if I hadn't been awake that very night, God would've found another time to put the idea in my brain or nudge me in a certain direction. When I'm being indecisive about something, I usually come to a decision in the wee hours of the morning. If your brain is backlogged with thoughts and worries that you don't have time to think about during the day, you're bound to think about them at night. Instead of letting your mind race at night, make better use of your time and take your thoughts to the Wonderful Counselor.

I'm sure He has the answers for you.

You just have to quiet your mind long enough to receive counsel.

But . . . I Need Sleep

You still need sleep; I know. And I'll be honest, this was a hard chapter for me to write because sleep is the biggest thing I still struggle with when it comes to my anxiety. Literally, nighttime and my anxiety are married or something. I could stay up all night, every night, if my anxiety had its way. But I'll give you a few pointers I've tried out, and you can see which (if any) you want to try.

Recently, I started an adult coloring book, and I work on it right before bed. I know it sounds juvenile, but it helps me wind down, and it's peaceful. I even got a devotional coloring book filled with Scripture! Of course, there are some nights where I don't color and I write instead (like tonight) because bedtime is when I get me time. But something like coloring, writing, or reading your Bible before bed may help you relax by the time your head hits the pillow.

Another suggestion I would make would be to limit your caffeine intake in the late afternoon. As I've already pointed out, I love my coffee. It's a must for this mama. It may not be for you, and that's fine; but I've made my choice in life, and I believe coffee is needed every morning. I rely on Jesus first and coffee second. Caffeine is a stimulant, and it perks us up every morning. However, its effects can last for hours longer than your third cup of reheated coffee. Caffeine has a half-life of about three to five hours, meaning after three to five hours, you still have half of the amount you consumed in your system. It can take much longer for it to be completely cleared from your system.[1] I was a barista in my college days and I'm going to let you in on a secret: decaf still has some "caf" in it. Even when you're not wanting a jittery jolt of caffeine, you'll still get a little bit in your system.

Bottom line, if you're like me and need your coffee, keep it to a cup in the morning and try to limit caffeine intake after one o'clock. (Okay, occasionally if I'm at Target, you'll see a Starbucks in my hand after one o'clock but definitely not later than three o'clock.) If you really like an afternoon pick-me-up, try tea. Even better, try Sleepytime tea before bed.

And my last suggestion for you would be to keep the serious conversations for another time instead of right before bed. I'm notorious for trying to have in-depth conversations with Billy right as he's trying to go to sleep. I can't help it. He works all day long, and I have all these topics I need to talk to him about. Plus, sometimes it's matters I can't discuss in front of the kids at the dinner table. So I start yacking his ear off right before bed, but really, it just stimulates me more and gets me thinking.

Like recently, the bedtime conversation revolved around kitchen remodel decisions, school options for William, and when we might want to start trying for baby number three. Talk about a heavy conversation right before bed. So what did my mind do? Well, I got to thinking about all those things, and I didn't sleep well that night. Too many decisions, too many thoughts, so little time, ya know? My advice—keep the big conversations for the morning or another time. You do it before bed and it's just going to get your brain racing.

The Stuff to Think About

- Are there certain things that trigger your anxiety more at night? Noises in the house or fear of losing sight of your kids? Remind yourself that God never sleeps. He's watching over you and your kiddos.

The Stuff to Try Out

- When you're awake at night, try talking to God about the worries you're obsessing about. See what He has to say about them instead of letting your mind bounce from one thought to the next. He'll either give you an answer or rock you back to sleep.
- Try some calming or relaxing techniques before bed. Read a book, read your Bible, or engage in some other peaceful and calming hobby that may help relax you. Also, try

limiting the serious conversations and save them for another time. They'll just get your mind going.

- Limit caffeine intake to mornings and try Sleepytime tea at night or some other calming, sleep-inducing supplement.

The Truth about It

> In peace I will lie down and sleep,
>   for you alone, LORD,
>   make me dwell in safety. (Ps. 4:8)

I will bless the LORD who counsels me—even at night when my thoughts trouble me. (Ps. 16:7 CSB)

9

I'd Like to, but My Anxiety Says No

(Feeling: My anxiety makes me avoid things or turn down things out of fear)

"How is the writing coming along?"

After I read the message a friend sent me, I texted back, "I'm avoiding writing the chapter about how my anxiety makes me avoid things . . . so about how I would expect."

Yeah, I sat on this chapter for a while. I avoided it for a few weeks. I don't know why this chapter was one I avoided—didn't seem like a hard topic. To be honest, though, I avoided the whole book. I have other books I've started, books about the messiness of motherhood and relying on Jesus through it all. You know, the lighthearted, humorous, encouraging type of book. But that's not the book God wanted me to write (maybe later, but for right now, this is the one). I've had numerous conversations about this book with Him.

Lord, this is not the book I want to write.

I told God to send someone else to write it and I believed there were other books already out there like this so mine didn't need to be added to the bookshelf. The first time I met my agent, I told her I had anxiety about my anxiety book (ironic, I know). It's not that I didn't want to help you with your anxiety; I did, and I do. This is a very personal, vulnerable part of my life, and the fear of judgment came to mind more than once. The fear of failure is persistent. The fear of bad reviews is not as persistent, but it's in the back of my mind. (Billy, if you're reading this, don't let me read the reviews! Got it? Good.)

But I truly believe everything I've been through has brought me here—typing these words out and sharing it all with you. My career dreams never involved writing a book. (At the age of thirteen, I submitted a piece to *Chicken Soup for the Preteen Soul*. It got rejected, and the short-lived dream died there.) However, when I took the leap of faith and quit my job (because of my anxiety, might I add), God placed a new dream in my heart. When He first began nudging me to write this book, I thought, *No way! I don't know how to write a book*. And yet, the first time I sat down to write, eight thousand words came out. *Eight thousand*. In the writing world, that's a lot. A lot of those words have not survived the Delete button, but it was still a sign to me that I definitely had a lot to share about this. There was a story there.

And I know a lot of you may not have been called to write a book (or maybe you have). A lot of you may have a fear of failure in general when it comes to anything in life. Maybe it's a new business idea you're thinking about pursuing. Maybe it's the desire to be a stay-at-home mom, but you're afraid of leaving your career behind or whether you'll be able to pick up where you left off when the kids grow up. Maybe it's a fear of a promotional opportunity because you feel more comfortable where you are right now. Maybe it's a fear of starting a small group at church or some kind of ministry. Maybe it's a fear of moving across the country and starting all over in a new town.

You want to know something? I've struggled with every single one of these fears. I've turned down a lot of opportunities or wrestled with saying yes to something until I'm worn down and have no other choice. I've worked overtime trying to impress my boss so I'd never have to sit through a poor performance review with her. I've tried people pleasing, and I've tried to do it all. I've grappled with the fear of failure more times than I can count. And I've struggled to take the steps to obey what God has called me to do.

I Don't Wanna—Please Send Someone Else

Let's take a look at Moses for a minute. In Exodus 3, we find Moses speaking to God through a burning bush. God has instructed Moses to bring the Israelites out of Egypt and lead them to the land that God will give to them, "a land flowing with milk and honey" (v. 8). Moses responds to God's instructions by saying, "*Who am I* that I should go to Pharaoh and bring the Israelites out of Egypt?" (v. 11, emphasis added). Moses has some serious doubts about his abilities.

God responds, "I will be with you" (v. 12).

We're going to pause a moment here in Moses's story to repeat that again: *I will be with you.* That was God's response to him when Moses felt like he was unqualified to do what God had called him to do. He was questioning whether God was calling the right person for the job, but God was like, "I'll be right there. Always."

Okay, now back to Moses's story. Moses had other questions he asked God, and God told him what signs He would perform so the Israelites would believe Moses and know who sent him. In chapter 4, we see some doubt again. Moses says, "Pardon your servant, Lord. I have never been eloquent, neither in the past nor since you have spoken to your servant. I am slow of speech and tongue" (v. 10).

Do you know how God responded to him this time?

"Who gave human beings their mouths? Who makes them deaf or mute? Who gives them sight or makes them blind? Is it not I, the LORD? Now go; I will help you speak and will teach you what to say" (vv. 11–12).

Hello, Moses! You may not have felt equipped, but God always is. God was not only *with* you but He would *help* you speak and tell you what to say. Moses's response?

"Pardon your servant, Lord. Please send someone else" (v. 13). Send someone else—I don't want to.

Moses was afraid to do what God called him to do. He was probably afraid of returning to Egypt (he had fled many years before after killing an Egyptian who was beating a Hebrew man). He didn't feel like he would be able to present himself well or that he would know what to say. I'm assuming he was afraid of failing, of letting God down, or of letting all the Israelites down. He wasn't a leader. He wasn't born a leader, but God called him to be one. Moses was dealing with some anxiety over what God was asking him to do.

God got angry with Moses for telling Him to send someone else, but God didn't disregard his feelings or cast him aside. He didn't send someone else. God instead sent Moses's brother, Aaron, with him to help speak for Moses. God didn't tell Moses he was worthless to Him because Moses didn't want to do what God commanded. And God didn't tell Moses he needed to get over his fear and just do it anyway. God sent someone else to help Moses, someone to boost his confidence a little bit. God still made sure Moses did the assignment He was calling Moses to do, and He still saw Moses through all of it.

What are *you* avoiding? What are you afraid of attempting to do because it makes you anxious? What ideas, dreams, or callings has God placed in your heart, yet you've come up with a whole list of reasons why you shouldn't do them? What reasons are holding you back? Fear of failure? Fear of judgment? Fear of not being good enough? Or is it fear of dealing with the anxiety of it all? (I know that would totally be me.)

Anxiety makes us avoid things that make us more anxious. Sometimes the things we're avoiding may be things we need to avoid, but more often than not, I'm betting they're missed opportunities. I'm guessing they're things God has called you to (for a reason) and your response is, "Send someone else." Or you're not even acknowledging that God has asked you to do it and you're pretending it wasn't a nudge by the Holy Spirit. You're just ignoring the call altogether. That's probably more likely, am I right?

Hebrews 13:20–21 puts it this way (and I'm adding emphasis so you can see where I'm going with this):

> Now may the God of peace, who through the blood of the eternal covenant brought back from the dead our Lord Jesus, that great Shepherd of the sheep, *equip you with everything good for doing his will*, and may *he work in us what is pleasing to him*, through Jesus Christ, to whom be glory for ever and ever. Amen.

God has control over all things, we know this. So when your anxiety starts telling you you're not enough when you're thinking about pursuing something, you may not be enough all on your own, but God is. When it comes to doing what God has called you to do but your anxiety is saying no, remember He will equip you to do whatever He's called you to. Every time you think the words, "I am not"—whether you mean "not talented enough" or "not smart enough"—God is everything you're not.

Hi, I'm Courtney, and My Anxiety Makes Me Awkward

"What is a fun thing in life you wish you would've done sooner?"

Yeah, I'm not answering that. Please don't look at me. Maybe I'll look at Billy, and he can answer for me. I hope this isn't like school where we all get called on by the teacher and I have to answer.

We were at a church small group gathering, and we were meeting these people for the first time. This was the icebreaker question to kick the group off. I had a lot of thoughts swirling around in my head, mainly about the kids (they're always at the top of my mind). I was worried about whether they were socializing well and making any friends with the other kids in the group. I had thoughts in my head of them being teased or not playing well with others. Or worse, thoughts of them being mean to another kid and being the bully. And to be honest, I get anxious in social settings with people I don't know.

But Billy and I knew our family needed to try a small group. The kids had not been in social settings with other kids, and Billy and I had not been around, well, anyone for a long time. Between him working from home and me being a stay-at-home mom, making friends was not something we could easily do. We also wanted to meet people who had the same values as us, and we wanted to create fellowship with other Christ-followers. So there we were, sitting quietly during the icebreaker and not saying a word.

What I wanted to say to the question was, "I wish I would've joined a small group sooner." That's how I should've responded, but then the question of "Well, why haven't you?" comes after that and the answer—my anxiety.

Social anxiety is totally a thing. Pits drenched in sweat, overthinking where the conversation will go, what to do if the conversation doesn't go anywhere and you're sitting there in awkward silence, stuttering over your words and hoping you don't sound weird, hoping you don't offend anyone with your jokes, not knowing what to talk about since you don't know what you have in common with the other people, feeling left out because everyone else knows each other and you're the new kid, not knowing what everyone will think of you, or even worse, thinking that everyone will hate you. Does this sound about right?

Oh, but wait, there's more. Three days after our first small group meeting I told Billy, "I Facebook friended a couple of the people we met at small group the other day." We were sitting at the dinner table and discussing our day.

"Babe, no. It's *way* too soon. You're going to come off as desperate and clingy," he responded as he face-palmed himself.

"You think?"

"Um, yeah!"

Great. I'm going to be the girl who's like, "Please, somebody, love me!"

Truth is, there is no easy way to make friends as adults. As kids, it's easy. We just run up to someone and say, "Hey, you want to be my friend?" and there you go. It happens so easily for them. There is no second-guessing anything. There are no social conventions or rules to making friends. You just go and be yourself. You don't worry about what others think of you because you're a kid; your parents have told you how wonderful you are. But as you get older, you learn not everyone is going to like you. You're not going to be everyone's cup of tea. Plus, if you have anxiety, you're going to constantly worry about whether you're doing or saying anything right, or if people are secretly judging you. You may be shy and uncomfortable with being around new people and have a persistent, irrational fear of social situations—whether you have a social phobia or a social anxiety disorder, it's a very real thing.

I don't have a social anxiety disorder, but I do struggle with feeling awkward around people I don't know very well. Once I get to know someone, though, I turn into a TMI, word vomit version of myself (kind of like the pages of this book). Whether you struggle with awkwardness or feel like social anxiety is something you have, let's look at some truths, shall we?

Looks aren't everything. Come as you are. I don't know about you, but when I'm meeting new people or in social situations, I tend to get stressed about my appearance. I worry about my outfit and if it's cute or if it makes me look pregnant. I worry about my hair and if it's a frizzy mess. I worry about making a good first impression, as I think a lot of people do. Well, here's the truth.

In 1 Samuel 16, we follow the prophet Samuel to Bethlehem as he has been called by God to the home of a man named Jesse. There Samuel will find the next king to anoint in order to replace King Saul, Israel's first king who has displeased God. Jesse has eight sons, and Samuel meets each one, waiting for the Lord to tell him who is to be chosen. God tells Samuel:

> Do not consider his appearance or his height, for I have rejected him. The LORD does not look at the things people look at. People look at the outward appearance, but the LORD looks at the heart. (v. 7)

God doesn't care about your appearance or that big zit you've got on your face that you're embarrassed about. Don't worry about what others think about it either, okay?

In the famous "Do Not Worry" message Jesus preached, He tells us in Matthew 6:25, "Therefore I tell you, do not worry about your life, what you will eat or drink; *or about your body, what you will wear.* Is not life more than food, and the body more than clothes?" (emphasis added). Even if you're wearing leggings and a T-shirt, if you're destined to make a real-life connection with someone, it's gonna happen. God places people in our lives for a reason. And look at it this way—you being real with others and wearing your normal apparel may allow you to connect with someone faster because they love leggings and tees too. Don't get all worked up about the little things. If friendship is meant to be, it's meant to be.

There's only One who truly judges you. Do you fear being judged by others? Unfortunately, it may happen. And if it does, it probably means they're not meant to be your new BFF. Also, first impressions can be deceiving, and someone may realize that and give you a second chance (or vice versa). Either way, if someone judges you, who cares? Their opinion of you doesn't matter. Only God's does.

> Do not judge, or you too will be judged. For in the same way you judge others, you will be judged, and with the measure you use, it will be measured to you.
>
> Why do you look at the speck of sawdust in your brother's eye and pay no attention to the plank in your own eye? How can

you say to your brother, "Let me take the speck out of your eye," when all the time there is a plank in your own eye? You hypocrite, first take the plank out of your own eye, and then you will see clearly to remove the speck from your brother's eye. (Matt. 7:1–5)

But I'd rather be a loner. I'm just a homebody. I like staying at home. I've always liked binge-watching *Gilmore Girls* or *Friends* (for the hundredth time) to, in a sense, live vicariously through the lives of the actors I watch on TV. There's less stress at home because I'm not having to worry about talking to people I don't feel like I have anything in common with. There's just me, Lorelai, and Rory (and maybe some mint chocolate chip ice cream). The problem with this is it's not good to be alone. God created us for relationships and friendships. It's how we thrive.

After God made Adam, He said in Genesis 2:18, "It is not good for the man to be alone," and along came Eve. God didn't create us to be loners. It may be easier on our anxiety to just stay home every day and not put ourselves into situations that make us anxious, but it's not His intention for our lives. If you're that much of a homebody, find someone else who's also a homebody and will sit around in sweats with you while binge-watching Netflix. I'll rephrase God's words for you: "It's not good for you to binge-watch alone."

I'm too much of a people pleaser. I think when it comes to anxiety, I get anxious about not pleasing others (perhaps you do too). I want to be liked. I want to do things well and be there for others. I want to appease others but end up stretching myself thin by trying to do all the things for all the people. I take on too much because I can't say no to anyone and disappoint them. Anxiety or not—*you* may struggle with people pleasing. And here's what God has to say about it:

Am I now trying to win the approval of human beings, or of God? Or am I trying to please people? If I were still trying to please people, I would not be a servant of Christ. (Gal. 1:10)

I think that's all there really is to say on this one; I've got nothing more for you on people pleasing.

Making friends as moms is hard. If you're a working mom, you have no time. If you're a stay-at-home mom, your day is lonely, filled with laundry and dishes. I've lived both lives as a mom, and I can tell you I had no social life. I've said no to social events as a working mom because I had no time to clean the house or grocery shop. I've awkwardly stood in the back at a library reading event as a stay-at-home mom and gazed around at all the other moms with a puppy-eyed look that said, "Please, friend me." I'm still stumbling my way through the awkwardness. I'm still nervously putting myself into situations that make me uncomfortable, praying I'll find someone to do Target runs with me (shopping is so much more fun with friends).

When it comes right down to it, if your anxiety makes you avoid social situations and you're nervous and awkward, the only way to face it is to embrace it. Laugh at yourself when you make the awkward comments. Embrace the messy attire and rock the mom look if it's what you're most comfortable in. Be yourself—every little bit of yourself that makes you so wonderfully you.

Don't let the fear of trying be the reason you don't find your people. Don't miss out on community and fellowship because your anxiety told you not to give it a go. Don't choose to shut down and not go to the MOPS group, the Mommy and Me group, or the small group meeting at church.

Face the fear. Embrace the awkwardness. Say hello to the nervousness.

And take that baby step.

The Stuff to Think About

- What does your anxiety make you avoid? Fear of failure? Fear of trying something new and taking a big step? Fear of social settings? It's time to embrace it and tell your anxiety that it's lying to you.

The Stuff to Try Out

- Embrace it and face it. Don't be afraid, and don't let your anxiety win. If God has called you to something, He'll see you through it. Start looking at those dreams or goals He's placed in your heart and look at some ways you can start pursuing them.
- If you struggle with social anxiety, try to do things that put you outside of your comfort zone. Join a small group at church or a local mom's group. Be yourself, embrace any awkwardness, and take the step toward finding true friendship.

The Truth about It

Now may the God of peace, who through the blood of the eternal covenant brought back from the dead our Lord Jesus, that great Shepherd of the sheep, equip you with everything good for doing his will, and may he work in us what is pleasing to him, through Jesus Christ, to whom be glory for ever and ever. Amen. (Heb. 13:20–21)

Am I now trying to win the approval of human beings, or of God? Or am I trying to please people? If I were still trying to please people, I would not be a servant of Christ. (Gal. 1:10)

I'm Just Over Here All by Myself

(Feeling: No one understands what it's like)

"Satan is inside of you. You need to fight him."

"There's nothing to be afraid of if you have faith."

"God didn't invent pharma. You don't need medication; you need more Jesus."

These are just a few of the types of comments I've gotten on some of my social media posts when I write about my mental health. I'll be honest—they hurt. I can't tell you how many times I've wanted to delete my blog page and walk away from it all because of how much these comments can hurt (and trust me, I've gotten more comments, even direct messages, like this). And I know these are from strangers on social media, so I shouldn't let them get to me! But I have a hard time not believing these lies as they're being spewed at me from strangers on the World Wide Web.

The truth is, these comments are just that—lies. They definitely can make a Christian who suffers from anxiety feel isolated. They can make a person start to doubt themselves and believe these lies.

And that's why I keep posting. Somewhere out there in the world, whenever I make a post, there is a mama who is believing all those lies. I need her to know she is not alone and shouldn't buy into the negative comments. And truth be told, for every hurtful comment I get on a post, I get another five comments or direct messages from women saying, "Thank you for sharing your story," or "I thought I was the only one who thought like this." My inbox is proof that you—and I—are not alone.

Whether you experience anxiety, depression, or any other kind of mental illness, you may already feel like you're not normal. (I've actually been told before that my thought process is not normal. It's fine. I'm fine.) You may already feel isolated because no one else understands what's going on in your mind or how your brain operates. But then, when you're a Christian with a mental illness, that's a whole other level of feeling not normal. When you're told "just pray more and trust God" instead of "that must be hard for you," or "I'd love to hear more about your story and struggles," you definitely don't feel the love. You start to believe there's a party for Jesus's very best friends, and you're not going to be invited because you were anxious you were going to die over a splinter you couldn't get out from under your skin (yes, that happened just last week). It's the feeling that every other Christian but you has a first-class plane ticket but because you occasionally can't turn your brain off from the worry, you're getting stuck in coach.

And you know what probably hurts the most? These are *Christ-followers* who are hurting you with their words—making you feel far from Jesus and isolated. These aren't just people who don't understand or are not educated about mental health but they're followers of Jesus who are supposed to be *the hands and feet of Jesus*. These are people who have committed their lives to love and serve Jesus but have failed to love their neighbor when their neighbor starts talking about what makes their heart race and cheeks flush. Instead, these people shame you. And maybe you've never been shamed by someone else. If that's the case, then yay! However, my guess is you have still felt isolated and alone with your thoughts. It's probably one of the reasons why anxiety's best friend is depression.

While this book is not focused on depression, I think it's important we take a quick look at it since the two often come together like a two-for-one kind of package deal. According to the National Alliance on Mental Illness (NAMI), "Some estimates show that 60% of those with anxiety will also have symptoms of depression, and the numbers are similar for those with depression also experiencing anxiety."[1] Read that again. *Over one-half.* (And as you've already read from my story, I am included in that number.) That means over half of the mamas whose hands are currently holding this book have struggled with depression at some point, are currently battling it, or may go on to develop it. This is the part where I tell you if you think you're struggling with depression as well, please speak to your doctor and seek the help of a mental health professional. Depression is a whole different beast on its own, and it's an ugly beast; trust me.

So which comes first, the anxiety or the depression? Someone with depression may feel anxious because of how hopeless and sad they feel. Someone with a social anxiety disorder may experience depression because of how much they've isolated themselves from others. Someone with anxiety may become depressed because of something they're worried or stressed about, making them feel hopeless. They may even become depressed because they feel like their anxiety makes them a failure. Anxiety can often pave the way for depression, and those who have a history of an anxiety disorder may go on to develop depression later. However, there is no evidence that one causes you to develop the other.[2]

Let's take a look at another biblical figure who experienced depression—the prophet Jeremiah. He's often called "the Weeping Prophet," and you'll see why in a bit. Jeremiah was destined to be a prophet. God set Jeremiah apart before he was even born. However, Jeremiah protested due to his doubts about his speaking abilities (much like Moses) and because of his young age (Jer. 1:6). Jeremiah was a prophet during a rough time in Judah. God sent him to warn the people of their future doom—Babylonian captivity—and urge them to repent of their sins and turn back to God. But they didn't listen to him.

Not only did the people not listen to him but they attacked him for the message he was delivering. First, the people of his hometown, Anathoth, plotted to kill him (Jer. 11:21). He was arrested and beaten multiple times (20:2; 37:15). He was mocked and ridiculed (20:7). A crowd of people attacked him as he was addressing them at the temple, and they demanded that he must die (26:7–11). And then he was thrown down a well (38:6).

That's a pretty rough life. Jeremiah was called to serve God even though he didn't want to. He preached and served a people he so desperately wanted to save from themselves, but they hated him. And then add a big factor to the mix—he was alone in all of it.

God commanded Jeremiah in chapter 16 not to marry or have children because God knew the soon-to-be future of His people. God also forbade Jeremiah from attending funerals to mourn the dead or comfort the bereaved. But that wasn't all. Jeremiah was also ordered not to socialize. No feasts and no parties. Now, that's some serious isolation. That's like if you were cut off from the world but you also weren't able to use FaceTime or social media. Plus, when you add on the fact that everyone was against him or out to get him, you can see how he came to be known as the Weeping Prophet. And what else do we see in Jeremiah's story?

Depression.

In Jeremiah 20:14–18 we get a look into the state of his mind with him cursing the day he was born, questioning why he was even born, and saying his life has been filled with only struggle and sorrow. Jeremiah (I'm assuming) didn't have anxiety, but he certainly experienced depression due to his circumstances and feeling like everyone was out to get him (because, well, they were). He never quit doing what God called him to do or speaking the words God put into his mouth, but I'm sure there were times when he wanted to. There are a few things we can take away from his story.

The first is no one is immune to anxiety or depression. We have a man who was loved by God and called to do His work, and he still struggled. He still experienced pain and sorrow in life. (We've already proven this point in this book, but here's yet another example of it!) And even though Jeremiah struggled, he still penned the very verse so many people with depression cling to when they're struggling. I'm sure you've read this one before but here's your reminder. "'For I know the plans I have for you,' declares the LORD, 'plans to prosper you and not to harm you, plans to give you hope and a future'" (Jer. 29:11).

The second thing we learn from Jeremiah is when you are cut off from others or when you feel like you have no one in your corner who is fighting with you, you're more prone to experiencing bouts of depression. However, even amid all of Jeremiah's struggles, he was never *truly* alone. God saw him through everything and kept him going, just as He does for you and me every day.

God does not want you to suffer alone. Jesus taught us that we are to love each other, as He loves us; this is His greatest command. We also learn from 1 Corinthians 12:12–31 that we are all many parts to one body—the body of Christ. The apostle Paul stressed the need for every part of the body of Christ to do their part and that there be no division amongst it. In verse 26, he writes, "If one part suffers, every part suffers with it." I also like The Message translation of this verse: "If one part hurts, every other part is involved in the hurt, *and in the healing*" (emphasis added).

I'm guessing since you've gotten this far in the book, you feel like your anxiety makes it harder for you to function every day. I'm guessing, like myself, you wouldn't just say you *have* anxiety but you *suffer* from anxiety because it can be debilitating some days. So where are your brothers and sisters in Christ as you are suffering? I'm guessing they're not suffering with you. I'm guessing they have strong opinions as to what you're going through. They may even be uncomfortable when you mention the word *anxiety* and try to deflect the conversation elsewhere.

Or perhaps you haven't told anyone. Perhaps this stigma has kept you silent for a long time. Perhaps you're too scared to tell anyone for fear you'll be judged and deemed a bad Christian.

Ugh.

That breaks my heart if that's the case for you. I don't know why some Christians are prone to make others feel like they are better Christians because they don't struggle with their mental health. Romans 15:7 reinforces that we should "accept one another, then, just as Christ accepted you, in order to bring praise to God."

We need to accept one another. No matter what.

Even if there are some Christians who never welcome you with open arms when you tell them you suffer from anxiety, know this—they struggle with other parts of their life too (they're just not open about it). It's a fact that we'll ALL have a form of suffering in this world. Just because we're believers does not mean we're given a ticket to an easy peasy life. I'm not sure why that means we have decided amongst ourselves which struggles and hard parts of life are okay to share with others and which to keep hush-hush. Unfortunately, no matter how many posts I make, I know there will always be some Christians who will still tell me my faith is the problem.

I want to talk about one other thing I get asked about a lot: what to do about significant others who don't understand your mental illness. It's something I want to mention, and if you're a single mama, you can skip the next two paragraphs. But there are a lot of women who do not feel supported by their significant others when it comes to their anxiety. Maybe you can relate; maybe you can't (and I'm praying you can't). However, maybe you've been told by your better half that you need to get over it or stop overthinking everything. I'll be honest, Billy didn't get my depression when we first started dating. He didn't get why I needed a pill to make me happy, and he thought that pill meant he wasn't enough to make me happy. He didn't understand the chemical imbalance going on in my brain. He wasn't aware of the war in my mind.

After some education, he gets it. He's seen it. He lives alongside me through it every day. He knows when I'm going through a depressive episode. He knows when I start snapping at him, it's my anxiety talking, not his loving wife. He's held me during a panic attack, and he's talked me down from my obsessive thoughts. My suggestion would be to educate your loved one. Have them meet your therapist and discuss your amygdala (sounds like a fun date night). Buy them a book that talks about the science behind your brain and the medical side of mental illness. Show them that you're not being difficult and a worrywart for nothing; there's more to it.

Just because those closest to you don't get your mental struggles, it doesn't mean they can't be taught. Just because others haven't spoken up, it doesn't mean they're not familiar with what you're going through. Just because some people shun you for having anxiety, it doesn't mean you're the only one dealing with anxiety. I wish it wasn't the case. I pray the number of those diagnosed with anxiety every year would go down instead of up. I wish it wasn't becoming so prevalent in our world, but it is.

And that's exactly why it's time we start talking about it.

I Have Anxiety! Praise Jesus!

Someone once commented on a post I'd written that announcing to the world that I'm a Christian mom who suffers from anxiety is not something to proclaim as if I'm proud of it. I'm not going to lie, I had mixed feelings about this comment. First, it hurt. Then, I started to question and doubt everything (because, you know, my anxiety made me have anxiety about what others thought about me, of course). However, if I stay silent about my struggles and how God has strengthened me through them, how am I ever going to glorify God for all He's done for me?

Yes, anxiety is the voice in my head that I wish I could shut up. However, if I shut up I'm not honoring God. I'm not helping others who have the same struggles, and I'm not bringing them closer to Him. I'm not helping others see how their suffering can be used for good, and I'm not helping them learn how to cope. And I definitely wouldn't be writing this book. Our good friend Paul puts it this way in 2 Corinthians 12:5, "I will not boast about myself, except about my weaknesses."

It's been a while since chapter 1, so let's revisit the whole basis for this book. We're looking for comfort for our anxiety so we can take our joy back in motherhood, right? (I mean, I know it's right, and hopefully I've been proving that point thus far.) Our greatest comforter is God; we know that. Again, in 2 Corinthians 1:3–4, Paul writes, "Praise be to the God and Father of our Lord Jesus Christ, the Father of compassion and the God of all comfort, who comforts us in all our troubles, so that we can comfort those in any trouble with the comfort we ourselves receive from God."

God is the God of all comfort, but just because He's comforting us, it doesn't mean the comfort stops there. We should be going out and comforting others with anxiety as well. We know what they're going through. We know better than anyone else what's going on in their brain. We're the experts on it because we live it every day. And wouldn't that mean we are able to give the greatest support to another mama (or anyone, really) who is battling anxiety? Even if it's just listening to what's going on in her mind, being able to share with someone else who struggles and will listen without judgment is huge!

Proverbs 12:25 reads, "Anxiety weighs down the heart, but a kind word cheers it up." (Fun fact: The Common English Bible reads, "Anxiety leads to depression," which means the Bible backs up what we learned earlier in this chapter—anxiety and depression are BFFs. The Easy-to-Read Version translation reads, "Worry takes away your joy," which we already know because that's what this book is focused on! Okay, now back to my point.) Anxiety weighs down the heart and can cause depression, but a kind word brings joy.

Be the kind word that will cheer someone else up. Spread the joy and be the one who makes a difference to another anxious friend or to anyone.

Here's another story to help back me up. In Luke 8:26–39, we see Jesus heal a demon-possessed man. (No, I am not comparing your anxiety to being possessed with a demon. I do not believe you are possessed, okay? Just clearing that up.) The man Jesus healed had not been wearing clothes for a long time and had been living inside the tombs. He immediately fell to the ground, crying out to Jesus when he saw Him. Jesus commanded the demons out of the man and sent them into a bunch of pigs that were feeding there on the hillside. The pigs rushed down the hill and into a lake where they drowned (gives a nice visual here that I wanted to add, totally not related to my point, though). The man wanted to go and follow Jesus, but Jesus said to him instead, "Return home and tell how much God has done for you" (v. 39). So the man went and told people all over town what Jesus had just done for him.

Of course, you may not have been healed from your anxiety (or had a demon removed and thrown into a pig). You may not have had a miraculous experience with your anxiety, and you may struggle every day to function because of it—but you *still* have a story to tell.

If you're currently struggling big-time with anxiety to the point that it's crippling, share the good news with others that Jesus is your greatest comforter and listens to all your worries. Share that He's walked this rough road with you and has never left you. Share the moments He has been with you and seen you through a panic or anxiety attack.

If you're in a good place with your anxiety (not yet healed but have a healthy method of coping with it), share the good news that Jesus sustains you through all of your worries. Share how He has worked through your counselor or doctor. Be the friend who will hold another friend's hand through all their worries and fears.

If you've been healed of anxiety (which I'm assuming may not be the case if you're reading this book, but who knows) share the good news with others and point them to Jesus.

Go and share your story.

I'm not saying you need to go out and start blogging about it like me or write a whole book on it (although you could). All I'm saying is staying quiet about it does not help anyone else. It does not praise Jesus for all He does and will continue to do in your life, anxiety related or not. You don't need to feel like you have to start telling your story to strangers; I'm not trying to give you something else to be anxious about. But I don't want you to feel like you need to hide your struggles from your family or even your friends. I get it; there's a stigma and fear of how someone will respond to you.

But do you know what? If someone shames you for opening up about your anxiety to them, I'm sorry, but shame on them, not you. Shame on them for making you feel like your mental illness is no big deal or a sign that you don't know how to pray. Shame on them for not loving their sister in Christ in her suffering. Shame on them for not being supportive like a good friend or family member should. And who knows, maybe you'll find they're uneducated on mental illnesses and they have no clue about the science behind it. If that's the case, you may be the very person who can inform them and help them adjust their response.

I won't lie; I still get anxious telling anyone about my anxiety and depression. Another thing I avoid is conflict because it makes me super anxious, and I'm always afraid of a confrontation with someone about my mental illnesses. However, they come up a lot these days whenever I tell someone I'm writing a book. (There's no way to avoid the topic of the book when you tell someone you're writing a book.) But I know when I tell someone about it and am met with love, that's someone I want in my corner. That's someone I know is going to be supportive and accept me as I am. That's someone who has made me feel heard. Seen. Loved. And *not* ashamed.

When you share your truth, you'll quickly find out who your real friends are; that's for sure. But what I can also guarantee is when you start talking about your anxiety, you're going to hear a lot of this: "Me too."

Yeah, when you start telling others about your anxiety, you're going to learn you're not as alone as you thought you were. You opening up is going to be the very thing that makes someone else feel brave, and they'll open up as well. And then guess what? You're not going to feel as isolated and alone in all of this! You're going to find even more comfort for your anxiety, and you're going to be able to share your struggles, hear another person's story, and praise Jesus for all He does for you. (Girl, preach it!)

When we all begin to share our stories and our suffering with others, we're going to be able to conquer that stupid stigma and break it once and for all. We're going to keep our eyes on Jesus and point others toward Him as the source of their comfort too.

Psalm 34:5 tells us, "Those who look to him are radiant with *joy*; their faces will never be ashamed" (CSB, emphasis added because keeping your eyes on Him will radiate joy from your face). The second part of this verse is interesting: You will never be ashamed.

Eyes on Him equals joy and no shame.

You really are not alone in this.

The Stuff to Think About

- When you tell someone about your anxiety, are you met with love or condemnation? Do you feel supported by others? If not, evaluate why. Are they not educated on mental illness? Inform them about the medical side of it. Did they take a biblical verse out of context that's led to their way of thinking? Redirect them to another Bible verse that breaks the stigma (this book is full of them).

The Stuff to Try Out

- Consider being more open about your anxiety and sharing what Jesus has done for you. Sharing your story may be what someone else needs, and you'll find you're not as alone as you thought you were.
- When you are unable to convince someone who has bought into the stigma, don't try to force it. Pray for them, and pray they won't judge you, but don't beat yourself up about it or get hung up on it. You know the truth, so don't forget it when lies are being spewed at you.

The Truth about It

Praise be to the God and Father of our Lord Jesus Christ, the Father of compassion and the God of all comfort, who comforts us in all our troubles, so that we can comfort those in any trouble with the comfort we ourselves receive from God. (2 Cor. 1:3–4)

Those who look to him are radiant with joy;
their faces will never be ashamed. (Ps. 34:5 CSB)

I Don't Need Help—I Have Jesus

(Feeling: Accepting medication or counseling means I'm weak)

I have a little scar on my left arm that's probably just over an inch long. It's more than twelve years old, so it's faded and not super noticeable to anyone who doesn't know it's there. If you did see it, you may think nothing of it. Could've been any kind of scrape or cut that left a scar on me.

But I know it's there.

I know what did it to me.

I did it to me—I put it there.

Before I go any further, you should know this was not a suicide attempt (although, yes, I had experienced suicidal ideation prior to this). The scar is on the top of my arm, and it was not deemed a suicide attempt because the cut would not have killed me—it couldn't.

The doctors called it "a cry for help." And that's exactly what it was. (And before I go any further, I have to say if you've had thoughts of suicide or harming yourself, please, please, *please* go seek the help of a professional. God does not want you to suffer alone—you are not alone. And He loves you.)

Maybe you've never struggled with suicidal thoughts or self-harm like I did in this moment, but my guess is you've had a "help me" moment where you've hit your breaking point. Maybe you've had one too many panic attacks and you've felt the nudge to seek help. Or maybe you've thought, "I need medication" or "I should talk to a therapist," but then the thoughts stop right there. Satan gets in your mind and whispers, "But you say you believe God is your healer. He must not love you or care about you if He hasn't healed you. Maybe He is punishing you. Maybe He's not even real."

Yeah, shut it, Satan.

Don't let your cry for help be a desperate plea like mine was. Don't let your "help me" moment leave a lasting scar, whether it's a scar on your body, like mine, or an emotional scar. Don't let your anxiety get so bad that you hit your breaking point. We all know how it ends for Satan, so tell him to shut it when he starts lying to you.

We're going to unpack Satan's lie bit by bit, but before we get started, I need you to keep an open mind. For whatever reason, when I talk about anxiety not being a sign of weak faith, people get all "Preach it, sister!" However, whenever I mention the words *medication* or *therapy*, people become judgmental and are no longer willing to hear me out. That is partially why this chapter is toward the end of the book. I figure by now you know enough about me, and you'll be a little more receptive to hearing me out instead of shutting the book. We all have differing views on modern medicine or therapy; I get it, and I'm not trying to change your view if that's the case for you. I just want you to keep an open mind and hear me out, okay?

Alrighty, here we go.

Thank You, Jesus, for the Gift of Doctors and Medicine

I went 172 days without leaving my house during the pandemic before I finally decided there was something I couldn't go without any longer. There was something I desperately wanted, desperately craved. I couldn't imagine other people getting to have it and not me.

A pumpkin spice latte.

That's right! It took PSL season to get me to come out of quarantine. It seemed like a simple thing. I would wear my mask, gloves, and it would be a quick drive-through trip then back home. *Nothing hard*, I thought. I'd done this hundreds of times before.

I got to the drive-through line, and I immediately started feeling my chest tightening and my heart racing. My face began to get hot and turn red, and I choked back tears as I got closer to the window. There was no escaping the line now; I couldn't back the car out or chicken out. I was stuck. I kept telling myself over and over again to calm down. *Be chill*, I thought. I didn't want to get to the window and be in tears as I was having an anxiety attack. I began reciting the Psalm 56:3 verse that I love so much. "When I am afraid, I put my trust in you."

I took deep breaths in and out. My heart began to slow down, and my hands were not as shaky when I got to the window. I stopped crying, but had some tears still in my eyes, so I apologized to the barista and said, "I'm sorry. I haven't done this since March."

She smiled at me (although she was wearing a mask, I could still tell it was a smile) and said, "Well, welcome back, friend!"

"Thanks," I said as the tears started coming again. This time it was tears of joy at what I had just accomplished.

I pulled to the side of the parking lot and had a conversation with God. I apologized for being so afraid of doing something that was so simple for everyone else but was debilitating for me. I realized how bad I was letting my anxiety get. I knew this had gotten way bigger than myself, and I couldn't do it anymore.

Courtney, it's time. Go get some help.

Well, you know there is no point in arguing with Him.

Okay, God. I'll make the call tomorrow.

That call, ugh. I immediately went into tears again with my doctor. "I've been off my medication for three years now. Everything was fine. I just . . . I feel like a failure," I said as I bawled.

And I did feel like a failure. I did feel like I should have been able to get better by myself. I felt like I should have been able to just rely on God, pray to Him, and He would heal me. I felt weak for taking medication and asking for help from anyone. I felt like doing so meant I'd failed in my relationship with God. It even planted the seed of doubt in me that God had failed me somehow. Don't get me wrong; God has gotten me through a lot of moments where a doctor or therapist would not have been able to help at all or make one iota of difference.

However, accepting help does not make me a failure. I'm not a failure. *You're not a failure.* Truth is, it takes such *strength* to admit you need help. It takes strength to accept the help. You're not a failure for taking it; *you're stronger for it.* Moms are notorious for not accepting help with anything, but your mental health is something with which you should not feel guilty about accepting help. And this is the part where I ramble to break this stigma.

If you had a headache, you'd take aspirin. If you had heart disease, you'd seek medication. If you had a rash on your arm, you'd get the medicated cream to make it go away. If you had diabetes, you'd take insulin. If you had appendicitis, you'd get your appendix removed. If you had difficulty seeing, you'd wear glasses. I could go on and on, but you get my point.

Before I go further, though, I want you to know that medication is not for everyone. This is not me telling you, "Go get some pills." This is just me saying there is a stigma about taking medication for mental illness, and I want to address that. I'm over here advocating for the treatment and use of medication. I don't know if medication would help you; I'm not your doctor. Your anxiety may not be a chemical imbalance and may be more manageable than mine. Counseling may be a better treatment option for you. I don't know. Either way, I'm just saying *it's okay* to have the conversation with your doctor if you think it may fit *your* circumstance and the level of anxiety *you're* dealing with. I want you to know there is nothing to be embarrassed about if you do decide to take medication.

If you don't want to have the conversation with your doctor or explore this option, that is okay too. I'm not trying to push pills on everyone. I just want people to stop shaming those of us who do take medication. Every time I have someone shun me for taking a little white pill for my brain, it breaks my heart. Medication and therapy saved my life from suicidal ideation all those years ago, and there is someone out there—this very moment—who is experiencing ideation as well. That person may be one pill away from their life being saved from suicide.

So even if you never agree with me on medication, I just ask that you don't judge others for taking a little white pill. Okay, enough preaching and now back to the stigma. Why is there a stigma around medication for mental illness? Why is it we don't call up the doctor right away and ask them to take care of it like we would for any of those ailments I described above? We've already discovered from chapter 1 that anxiety is in fact an illness, so what's the deal? What do people have against medicine and doctors when it comes to our brains?

I'm gonna be blunt here. Christianity and science don't always agree. I'm not sure when the two became so divided (my guess is when the idea of evolution came about), but I believe the two can work together. I also believe God uses doctors and medicine to heal us. I believe it's a gift from God, and it is *His healing hands* at work through others. Here's why I believe this.

The Gospel of Luke (my favorite of the Gospels) is a very detailed, "carefully investigated" account of Jesus's life (Luke 1:3). Luke also wrote the book of Acts. He wasn't just a dedicated co-worker of Paul's—he was also a physician. Paul refers to Luke as "the doctor" (Col. 4:14). And in Luke 14:2, Luke uses the Greek word *hudrópikos*, which is a medical term that means "suffering from edema" and doesn't appear anywhere else in the Bible.[1] Luke's medical background may also be the reason why Luke was the only one who mentioned Jesus's blood-like sweat in the garden of Gethsemane.

Jesus also healed. A lot. However, He sent His disciples out to heal in His name too. In Luke 9:1–2 we read, "When Jesus had called the Twelve together, he gave them power and authority to drive out all demons and to cure diseases, and he sent them out to proclaim the kingdom of God and to heal the sick." Peter healed a man who could not walk in Acts 3, Ananias healed Paul (then Saul) and restored his sight in Acts 9, Paul healed a man who could not walk in Acts 14, and Paul healed another man who suffered from a fever and dysentery in Acts 28. And people carried the sick out to the streets, laying them on mats and lining them up for the apostles to heal them in Acts 5.

Even in the Old Testament, others healed on God's behalf. Elijah healed a widow's sick son who had stopped breathing in 1 Kings 17. The prophet Elisha healed a man named Naaman of leprosy in 2 Kings 5. Isaiah told Hezekiah to "prepare a poultice of figs" after God answered Hezekiah's prayer to heal him in 2 Kings 20. All of them were not God but still healed on God's behalf with His power or healed through the knowledge God had given them.

I know what you're thinking—they're all apostles or prophets, men who had super close relationships with God. They all performed miraculous healing in the name of God, and that's not the same as comparing them to a doctor who uses medicines and surgical procedures. Okay, here's another point. In 1 Corinthians 12:4–6, Paul explains spiritual gifts: "There are different kinds of gifts, but the same Spirit distributes them. There are different kinds of service, but the same Lord. There are different kinds of working, but in all of them and in everyone it is *the same God at work*" (emphasis added). Different kinds of work, but it's all God's work. And why does God give us spiritual gifts? Paul answers that in verse 7: "A spiritual gift is given to each of us so we can help each other" (NLT).

So we can help each other. Doctors (and therapists) are there to help us, right?

Okay, I'd like to dig into the different kinds of gifts a little further to prove my point. In verse 9, Paul writes, "To another *gifts* of healing by that one Spirit." I added emphasis here to show you that the word "gifts" is plural, not singular. This means there are multiple methods of how one could heal another, and there are many different kinds of healing gifts that the Spirit gives.[2] Paul also describes the gift of knowledge in verse 8, and he describes another gift of "miraculous powers" in verse 10. My personal belief is that miraculous powers and gifts of healing can be (or are) separate. Jesus and His apostles performed miraculous healing, but Paul names them as two separate gifts. So I believe not all healing may happen in a miraculous way but in many different ways.

What do I want you to take away from all this?

God gives doctors the gift of medicine, knowledge, and healing. Period. Anxiety is highly treatable. However, of those diagnosed with an anxiety disorder, only about 37 percent actually receive treatment.[3] That means *more than half* of those with anxiety are suffering all on their own, and sadly, a lot of them probably don't rely on God to help them through it either.

My hope is you'll consider having a conversation with your doctor if you feel like it's the right decision for you. I'm not going to lie; not every medication is a perfect match to your brain's chemistry. It's like dating—you may have to try a few medications before you find the right one. I won't get into all the different kinds of medications available. I'll leave that conversation for you and your doctor. But I will tell you from experience, it won't always take away all the symptoms of your anxiety. It's not going to be a 100 percent effective fix. I said anxiety was *highly treatable*, not necessarily curable. But if you can find a medication that helps, and you pair it with therapy, those two methods together may create the miracle you've been praying for.

You may not need it for very long either. It doesn't have to be a forever pill. There may be times in your life where your anxiety is debilitating so medication is necessary, and there may be times when you're doing just fine without medication. That's okay.

It's okay to seek help and try medication if that's what your doctor thinks will help.

It's okay to feel weak and accept that you're not doing okay fighting it all on your own.

It's okay to not have it all together all the time.

It's okay to be a mom who takes medication for her anxiety.

Let's be honest, your kids need their mama feeling her best, and sometimes that means seeking help and putting your mental health first.

Thank You, Jesus, for Therapists

"So I was trying to get the straw carefully out of the paper wrapper so I could put it into the cup. But as I was doing it, my hands touched the tip of the straw, and of course, my hands weren't washed or sanitized. Well, I *really* wanted my iced coffee, and my anxiety kind of went through the roof. I really, really wanted my coffee, though. So I found a little thing of baby sanitizer in the car, took it and I sprayed the tip of the straw where my mouth goes . . ."

I looked up at her, expecting to see judgment. (Yeah . . . I was afraid of germs and sprayed sanitizer on a straw. I told you, I really love my coffee. It was vanilla-scented sanitizer, so it enhanced the flavor, I guess?) My counselor didn't seem surprised by it, and all I could do was laugh at myself and the absurdity of what I did. I'm sure she's heard way more than that from others. She talks to people who suffer from anxiety all the time. I'm sure I'm not the first person to do something completely off the charts like that. And you know what? I felt *relief* from telling someone else about the thought process in my head and the things it makes me do. Sure, I had told this story to Billy and didn't receive judgment (well, maybe a little bit of judgment, but he's vowed to love me in sickness and in health). But it was so nice to tell a stranger who doesn't know me very well as well as explain my anxiety to her.

It is nice not to feel judgment or embarrassment when you tell someone else something personal like your anxious thoughts—it's such a relief. Talking to someone helps tremendously, but that's not all my counselor does for me. We're able to talk through my thought patterns and figure out strategies to reverse the thoughts, to combat them and change the path my brain goes down. She gives me suggestions and other tips and tricks I can work on. But a lot of it is talking about my anxiety and rationalizing this brain of mine to myself. And no, my head is not being "shrunk" by a "shrink."

I think that's a big reason a lot of people avoid therapy—the stigma that you must be crazy if you're going to therapy.

Here's the truth to that lie: you are not crazy. Sure, you get worked up about nothing and your body starts to think it's in danger when it's not—but you're not crazy. No one with a mental illness is crazy. They've got a brain that's just a bit different than others. Or they've gone through a lot in this hard world, and those struggles have led to more struggles. But, no, you're not crazy. Regarding the stigma around therapy, I'm going to do a nice little rambling list again like I did for taking medication, so here it goes.

If you're looking for spiritual guidance, you go to your pastor. If you're sick with a physical ailment, you go to your doctor. If you're struggling with your mental health, you go to a mental health professional. There should be no reason why you can't see a therapist for your anxiety if that's the treatment you feel is best for you.

Yes, Jesus is our Wonderful Counselor, and the Holy Spirit is our Advocate and Counselor. However, there is no shame in getting counsel from others either. Obviously, test your therapist's guidance against Scripture and seek further guidance from the Spirit. Don't let your counselor steer you in the wrong direction by any means. But receiving support and further treatment from a mental health professional does not make you a weak Christian.

(There are actual Christian mental health professionals, which I'll talk about in a minute.) Scripture backs me up on this.

> Pride leads to conflict;
>> those who take advice are wise. (Prov. 13:10 NLT)

> Without good direction, people lose their way;
>> the more wise counsel you follow, the better your chances. (Prov. 11:14 MSG)

> Counsel in a person's heart is deep water;
>> but a person of understanding draws it out.
>> (Prov. 20:5 CSB) (And remember what "heart" also means in Hebrew—your mind.)

Solomon was a wise man (as well as the author of Proverbs), and a wise man (or woman, in this case) isn't afraid to seek counsel from other wise men or women. Also, it is very possible that God could speak to us through counselors or therapists. God used prophets and prophetesses to speak to His people in the Old Testament days. God uses pastors, teachers, friends, even strangers every day to speak to us. So why can't He use a therapist to speak to us and send a message our way? The Holy Spirit is not limited. God has no limitations for how He talks to us, when He talks to us, or how He heals us.

So what kind of options do you have available to you as far as mental health professionals? I'll tell you my experience first and then give you a little insight into other options.

When I struggled with depression as a teen, I can't tell you how many therapists I saw—from psychiatrist to psychologist and everything in the middle. However, as an adult seeking treatment for anxiety, I've tried two different options. Much like medication, this is also like dating, and sometimes it takes a while to find the right fit. So don't be afraid to try a few different therapists before you decide who you like best.

For my anxiety, I first tried seeing a mental health coach. Honestly, I tried this option first because it was a free option through my insurance plan. Mental health coaches differ from therapy because they are very goal-oriented, and they don't treat your anxiety as an illness. They are there to help you stay motivated, support you, guide you, and hold you accountable to your action items. Coaching is more focused on future goals, whereas therapy is focused on past and present.[4] The coach I met with was through a text-based app, so ultimately, I didn't feel like it was a good fit for me. I personally prefer talking with someone; it feels like I'm able to accomplish more in an hour versus typing all the words out through text messages. Even though the texting was nice because I could message my coach during Adelyn's nap time, it just wasn't working for me. (But it could for you!)

So after trying a mental health coach, I sought the help of a licensed professional *Christian* counselor. (Yes, that's a thing!) I chose a Christian counselor because she is a licensed counselor who uses the same methods as any other counselor and therapist, such as cognitive behavioral therapy (CBT). She has all the knowledge of psychology and the inner workings of my brain, but she also shares my faith with me, refers to Scripture, and I can freely talk to her about my faith. She bridges the gap between therapy and my faith in every session, and that is important to me.

If you're not concerned about having a Christian counselor specifically (and that's okay!), there are so many different options available to you. Psychiatrists, psychologists, counselors, clinicians, therapists, clinical social workers, and mental health coaches—you have a ton of options. I won't get into what all the differences are; I'll let you do your own research to find the right fit. But a lot of the differences are related to education, credentials, and what level of treatment is provided. You can check with your church and see if they have any recommendations (that's how I found mine), or you can check with your insurance company.

You're probably wondering, *When do I have time to do this?* (I know it's crossed your mind.) If you're a stay-at-home mom, you don't get a moment to shower, let alone spend an hour at a counselor's office. If you're a working mom, you're at work. You may not have a flexible schedule or a flexible boss, and you can't get away for an hour every week or even every other week. You may even feel embarrassed for telling your boss you need to take a long lunch or something because you don't want them to ask what it's for. I get it.

I think it's a mom thing. We feel guilty trying to sneak away to do something for ourselves. We feel guilty even asking for a break, so asking for something like this is hard. Luckily, we do live in a world now where virtual or telehealth visits are becoming a big thing, so it is possible to attend therapy and not leave your house. Even if virtual is not an option for you, there is still no need to feel guilty or humiliated by needing to see a therapist.

Do not feel guilty for asking someone to watch the kids during the day so you can prioritize yourself and go to an appointment. Do not feel guilty for talking to your boss about your schedule and seeing what you can work out so you can attend a session. And if your boss fights you on it, go get a note from your doctor or therapist (taking care of your mental health is taking care of your overall health).

The point is to prioritize yourself and put your mental health first. Seek the treatment because it's available to you and anxiety is highly treatable. Seek your joy because you deserve it.

Your mental health matters.

The Stuff to Think About

- What's kept you from seeking the help of a professional? Shame? Feeling like a failure or feeling weak? Finding the time to actually go to therapy? Identify what it is and pray about it. Pray for direction on if you should seek treatment or what sort of treatment you need.

The Stuff to Try Out

- If you feel like medication may be a step for you to take, try calling your primary care doctor or visiting a psychiatrist. Just remember, finding the right medication may take time. Be patient; you'll find the right one. Also remember it's not going to make all of your anxiety go away (and especially not overnight), but it will make your anxiety more manageable.
- If you feel like therapy is the next step for you, reach out to your church for suggestions or call your insurance company. Do some research on the options available to you and see which would be the best fit for you. Don't be afraid to meet with a few professionals before you find the best choice for you.

The Truth about It

> Without good direction, people lose their way;
> the more wise counsel you follow, the better your
> chances. (Prov. 11:14 MSG)

12

You Have My Eyes, but I Don't Want You to Have My Anxiety

(Feeling: I'm afraid my kids will have anxiety)

"Hey, buddy, are you excited for the dentist tomorrow?"

"No, I'm a lil bit scared," William responded to me.

"Well, what are you scared about? Let's talk about it."

"I don't know. I haven't decided yet," he responded.

Sounds about right, I thought. *Welcome to my life.*

To be fair, it was his first time to the dentist in two years, and he had no memory of going. He also was only four years old so indecisiveness and being afraid of things were just a part of everyday life at that age. But one thought has always been in the back of my mind.

I don't want my kids to grow up to have anxiety.

Forget developing anxiety when they grow up, they can have it at their current age. I've already seen the signs. I'm well versed in the signs because I've lived through them my whole life. There are more and more children being diagnosed with anxiety these days. Childhood anxiety is a real thing, and some therapists are treating children as young as three years old. Plus, when you add in the fact that anxiety *can be* genetic, chances are one or both of my kids will be like Mommy and have anxiety.

It's a hard truth to read, I know.

Here's why I think it's becoming more prevalent in our world today when it comes to our kids and anxiety: pressure. Kids these days have a significant amount of pressure put on them. Pressures about school, grades, extracurricular activities, getting into college. We're expecting them to read in kindergarten (for whatever reason), and we're expecting more and more from them at such a young age. Then you have bullies and the fear of not making friends. Then you have this scary world and fear of school shootings or terrorist attacks. I could go on and on. It's leading to an epidemic of childhood anxiety. According to the Centers for Disease Control and Prevention (CDC), "9.4% of children aged 3–17 years (approximately 5.8 million) had diagnosed anxiety in 2016–2019."[1] And that's a prepandemic statistic!

As a mom who has anxiety, you don't want your children to break from the pressure or to suffer from fear of this world. You sure don't want them to experience all that you have. You can't stand the thought of them struggling with anxiety like you. Watching your children being fearful may make you feel helpless and probably more anxious. (If having anxiety about having anxiety is a real thing, then anxiety about your kids having anxiety is for sure a thing too.) You want nothing more than to take away the fear for them.

You want to fix it all for them because that's what mamas do.

The Warning Signs

"When I couldn't do sleepovers as a kid . . . did you ever think that was anxiety?" I texted my mom as I was reflecting on my childhood and preparing to write this chapter.

"Yes . . . you couldn't separate yourself from me or home, your security. But once you were in college after your first year, you couldn't wait to get away from me. So I guess you overcame it," she texted back. (I detected a hint of sarcasm from her because I now live thousands of miles away from my mama.)

I had a lot of signs of anxiety as a kid, but back in those days, childhood anxiety wasn't as well-known or talked about. As a mom with anxiety, though, I know the signs, and I have kept an eye out for them. Maybe you didn't experience anxiety as a kid, so let's list out a few ways child anxiety differs from adult anxiety.

Toddlers go through an array of fears as they're learning all about the world, and a mama knows how to calm down a kid for fear of monsters in the closets, weird noises, and (my favorite) the shadows on the walls. So when does it go from being a normal, childhood fear to an anxiety diagnosis? According to the CDC, "When children do not outgrow the fears and worries that are typical in young children, or when there are so many fears and worries that they interfere with school, home, or play activities, the child may be diagnosed with an anxiety disorder."[2]

What exactly could that look like for a child? It could be separation anxiety and not being able to leave Mama's side (which is normal until they hit a certain age). It could be social anxiety and fear of playing with other kids or making new friends. It could be a severe phobia or fear of something else that's totally out there. Or it could be just fear and worry about things that a typical child shouldn't worry about.

Here's a problem. Your child may not know how to articulate their fears or emotions. Because of that, their anxiety may manifest as tantrums, acting out, arguing, or seeming completely distracted. Sure, they could appear to be visibly shy or clinging to you for dear life if they're put into a situation that makes them anxious. But a lot of the time, a young child who does not recognize their own emotions is going to come off as difficult to you. They're going to be the kid kicking and screaming because they're overwhelmed and they're trying to avoid the thing that's making them anxious. As a result, you're going to be completely overwhelmed (and anxious too).

That's the face of childhood anxiety.

Is it your child?

My Fears Becoming Their Fears

"What's that?" William asked me.

"Um, it's a security system. It's kinda like Toodles," I replied. (Toodles is from *Mickey Mouse Clubhouse*.) Seemed like the best way to describe the new security system we put in. (The system alerts you any time a door opens and talks to you, you know, like Toodles might.)

I knew I couldn't be like, "It's to keep bad people from coming into the house and stealing you in the night," or "It's going to hopefully make it easier for Mommy to sleep." I don't want my fears to become their fears. That's the tricky thing about motherhood. You want to make sure your children are aware of "stranger danger" and won't get into that strange van when asked. You want to make sure they're aware of the hazards of electrical sockets so they don't stick something in there. You want to make sure they don't eat the dishwasher pod (yeah, it's happened a couple times) and are aware of the dangers of this world. It's the same reason our kids go through fire drills, active shooter drills, tornado drills, and earthquake drills—to prepare them and teach them what to do in the event of danger.

However, as a mom with anxiety, I find it hard to distinguish between preparing or teaching children and scaring or passing the baton that is your anxiety to them. It's hard to teach your kids not to be so afraid when you're living with fear every day. So how do we manage and make sure our anxiety isn't making them anxious too? I have a few suggestions.

Is the thing you're about to tell or teach them something you're only anxious about, or is it a rational thing? This kind of goes back to rational versus irrational fears, like we talked about in chapter 2. Are you talking to your kids about something only you are afraid of, or are you really preparing them for something any other kid their age would need to know about?

Share just the right amount of information. Go through the facts of whatever fear your child is experiencing, but don't over-share or start listing the scenarios you've played out in your mind. Stick to the basics, and don't overindulge them (unless they're asking for more—then still tread carefully).

When your kids come to you with something they are afraid of, speak truth to them. Remind them what God has to say about fear and remind them that you and God are watching over them and will protect them. If their fear is extreme or make-believe (like many childhood fears are), be the voice of reason for them. You are their safe house and their biggest comfort.

When you're experiencing high levels of anxiety and you're having a hard time hiding your emotions, be honest with your kid. You can be open about your anxiety and your feelings without going into too much detail and causing them to be afraid of the same things. "Mommy has anxiety, and it causes her to be scared sometimes." Let them know it's okay to experience those feelings and emotions so if they one day start feeling the same way, they know to tell you so you can help them.

Anxiety can be contagious in a sense, especially when we're talking about children with active imaginations. But there is no reason for your fears to become their fears. You don't have to pass on the worry to future generations. When it comes to things that scare you or heighten your anxiety, you can still be open and honest without sharing too much and making your kids scared as well.

Mama's anxious, but it doesn't mean your kids have to be too.

Mommy Knows All about This

"And I would be putting her into preschool or do story time at the library soon to help with this anxiety," the doctor shouted to me as

Adelyn was freaking out. (She had to raise her voice because that's how loud Adelyn's screams were.)

"Okay, thanks," I said as I tried to hold back the tears and console Adelyn at the same time.

Adelyn had been to the doctor before; this wasn't new to her. She wasn't even getting a shot this time around. However, this trip to the doctor with her was way different than any other visit. I had to literally pin her down for the doctor to get a peek into her mouth and ears. I don't even know if I could technically say she got a full exam with the amount of flailing this girl was doing. She didn't like anyone touching her. She didn't like that I made her take her shoes off. She didn't like someone trying to poke and prod her belly. Girl was mad. Total flip out mode.

It was complete stranger danger at its finest. Pretty typical for a young toddler, especially when Mommy is a stay-at-home mom, and the toddler doesn't go to day care or interact with others much. This behavior definitely had me worried. When the doctor used the word "anxiety," I prayed, *Please, Lord, no. I pray she doesn't have my anxiety.*

And then there was William.

"Please, buddy, let me put your clothes on!"

"No! I don't wanna go! I'm not going!" he shouted at me.

"Honey, can you hold him down over there?" I asked Billy as we were pinning William down, trying to get him dressed so we could take him to the hair salon.

"I'm not going! I don't wanna!" was all William could scream.

It should've been a simple thing. I had been cutting his hair for quite a while, and it was time for someone else to do it (and for it to actually look good). The kid did not want to go. It was scary and new for him, and he was not having it. I just wanted to cry, and I felt like such a bad mom. Simple things—outings, meeting new people, going to new places—scared my kids, and I was afraid they were developing anxiety as well.

I have to tell you this chapter was hard for me to write (and probably why it's the shortest chapter in this book). I've volunteered to share my story, but that doesn't mean I need to share all the struggles my family has faced along with me. Without telling you every detail, I'm going to tell you this: If you ever do need to seek treatment for your kid's anxiety, you're the parent, and you control the narrative.

If you're nervous about your kid and feel like something is wrong with them or you're afraid of the stigma, you can make it feel as normal as going to the pediatrician or the dentist. There is no shame in seeking treatment, and you control what your child thinks about it all.

Getting your child help doesn't mean they will have anxiety for life either. It very well could be circumstantial and something they'll outgrow, or they could end up struggling more as an adult. Who knows? You don't have insight into the full workings of their brain. Their anxiety could be situational or their DNA could've been heavily influenced by yours. Only God knows. Maybe you are an adoptive mom, and your genes are not a factor; it is still possible your child could develop anxiety. You just don't know, but there's no point in being anxious about it. That would mean worrying about the future, and we already know whose hands hold that.

The point I'm trying to make is just because you struggle with anxiety, it doesn't mean you have to watch your kid struggle too. If your child does experience anxiety of any form (social, separation, phobia, general), you know what it is they're going through. You also know treatment can help them. (And maybe you don't know because you haven't sought treatment yourself yet. But it can help your kid. Even for young kids, play therapy can be very effective.) You know your child better than anyone else, and you shouldn't be afraid to get them the help they need.

No stigma—that right there is the truth of it.

I have completely normalized my mental illness to my kids. They have watched me take my medication—I don't hide it in the cupboard or anything. They've asked what it is, and I've told them,

"It's one of the ways God helps Mommy with her anxiety." I've told them about therapy and how my counselor is "Mommy's feelings friend" who helps me talk about my feelings and deal with them. I make anxiety normal for them, and I break the stigma. I make sure they know they can always come and talk to me if they ever start feeling anxious or depressed. There is no need to fear your child being labeled with anxiety or what other people will think. For your kid, it's all about helping them to cope early on and getting the help they need.

According to the CDC, "6 in 10 children (59.3%) with anxiety received treatment" in the year 2016.[3] Yup, that's a higher percentage of kids getting treatment for anxiety compared to adults! Why is that? I think adults with anxiety feel like they can handle it all on their own and deal with it. The other likelihood is when it comes to our kids, we just can't handle their anxiety. It's too huge for us to deal with on our own, and we need help. Either way, it gives me hope that the stigma around mental illness is being beaten. It tells me that this younger generation is being better educated around mental health and they won't be ashamed to seek treatment.

We're raising the future generation here. If there has been a stigma for so long about mental health and getting help for it, we're the ones who have full control over breaking the stigma by how we raise our kids to think and feel about it all. We can normalize mental illness and raise our kids to believe it is completely normal to seek help for it. I would much rather my kids see me in my struggles while I rely on God through it all and get the help I need than have my kids believe mental illness means I'm a crazy person and it's something we don't talk about as a family. I want them to come to me if they ever struggle—with anything.

To be honest, I don't have much more for you regarding this topic. As I type this out, my kids are still in the "littles" season, and I'm still learning as I go, just like anyone else experiencing motherhood. Plus, this book is about your anxiety, and childhood anxiety is a book topic on its own.

I just want you to know this: If your kid does end up having anxiety or if they experience it as a young child, you're their biggest advocate because you know what they're going through. You know exactly what it's like, and you know exactly how to help.

The Stuff to Think About

- Have you seen any signs of anxiety in your child? How have you approached the subject with your kid? Does your child even know you have anxiety, or have you hidden your struggles? Know the warning signs of childhood anxiety and how it can manifest differently than your anxiety.

The Stuff to Try Out

- Childhood anxiety is becoming common in our world, especially with the amount of pressure we place on our kids these days. As the parent, you can control the pressure they're feeling, and you can ensure they're not getting overly anxious about things like getting into college and the future.
- When it comes to your fears, you can express things and prepare your child without making your child anxious or overly scared. There is a way to balance it and not pass your anxiety down to them.
- Don't be afraid to get your child help if you feel like they have anxiety and it's affecting their everyday life. There is no need for you or your child to be humiliated about anything.
- Normalize mental illness for your kid. Don't be afraid to share insight into your struggles (age-appropriate insight,

of course). That way, if your child ever struggles, they will feel comfortable coming to you. Your child may not have anxiety, but they very well could. Don't be afraid to seek help for your kid if needed.

The Truth about It

> Trust in the LORD with all your heart
>> and lean not on your own understanding;
> in all your ways submit to him,
>> and he will make your paths straight. (Prov. 3:5–6)

> He tends his flock like a shepherd:
>> He gathers the lambs in his arms
> and carries them close to his heart;
>> he gently leads those that have young. (Isa. 40:11)

Conclusion

She Took Back Her Joy

I'm going to venture a guess that you're still feeling anxious. Am I right? You've read fifty-some thousand words on anxiety and God's truth about it all, but I'm guessing you're still not cured. Well, I never labeled this book as a "how to be healed from anxiety" book. What I promised was that we were going to journey together to search for comfort and not let anxiety steal our joy. Did we accomplish that? Maybe not yet, but I'm praying this last section hits my point home!

Okay, so here's another little story from the Bible that may bring you some comfort. In Matthew 14:22–33, we read the story of Jesus walking on water (a story I'm sure you're familiar with or one you've at least heard about). The disciples were in a boat and Jesus was praying on land. The boat had been knocked about by the wind and had started to drift away from shore. Jesus walked out on the water to the disciples, who in a panic said, "It's a ghost" (v. 26).

"Take courage! It is I. Don't be afraid," Jesus said to them (v. 27). (Seriously, by this point, the disciples had already witnessed Jesus perform many other miracles, so why it was a surprise to them that He could walk on water, I'll never know.)

"Lord, if it's you," Peter replied, "tell me to come to you on the water" (v. 28). Jesus told him to come. Peter climbed out of the boat and began to walk on water toward Jesus. However, when he saw the wind, he got afraid and started to sink. He cried out to Jesus to save him.

Jesus was literally right there.

Peter, sweet Peter, who loved Jesus so. The Peter who would become one of the first leaders of the early church. The same Peter who followed Jesus with such faith and passion, vowing he would never leave Jesus, and yet still managed to deny Him three times before the rooster crowed—yeah, that Peter. Peter was standing right in front of Jesus, and he was *still* afraid.

Come on, Peter! He's right there! Why on earth would you be scared?

This goes to show that just because he was a disciple of Christ and spent years following Jesus and listening to His teachings, it didn't make him immune from fear completely, right? Same reason he denied knowing Jesus three times: fear for his life. We could get into Peter's doubt, and we could talk about how his eyes left Jesus and how he got distracted by the wind and waves, but that's not the point I'm trying to make with this story. My point is Jesus caught Peter when he started to sink.

In Peter's fear, Jesus reached His hand out and grabbed Peter. Jesus could've been like, "Well, you took your eyes off Me, so there you go. You're going to sink now, and I hope you know how to swim." Totally does not sound like our Jesus, right? Not even close. The wind and waves whipped about, and Jesus reached His hand out to grab Peter.

He's a hand-holder, no matter what.

I recently read a portion of a psalm that I really loved, and I want to share it with you:

> Yet I still belong to you;
> you hold my right hand.

You guide me with your counsel,
    leading me to a glorious destiny.
Whom have I in heaven but you?
    I desire you more than anything on earth.
My health may fail, and my spirit may grow weak,
    but God remains the strength of my heart;
    he is mine forever. (Ps. 73:23–26 NLT)

No matter what, God is the strength of your heart, including your mind. No matter what, He will counsel you and lead you. No matter what, you still belong to Him and He's going to hold on to your hand.

No matter how many nights you lie awake tossing and turning with worry or how many panic attacks you have.

He'll hold your hand through it all.

No matter how many times He tells you to stop worrying about tomorrow but you still worry about it.

He'll hold your hand through it all.

God reminds us in Isaiah 41:13,

For I am the Lord your God
    who takes hold of your right hand
and says to you, Do not fear;
    I will help you.

He's not going to let you sink and drown in your anxiety as long as you turn to Him and seek His help.

Take His hand.

He's offering it to you so go ahead and grab it.

My Anxiety Can Be Pretty Bossy

Let me tell you, I used to use my anxiety as an excuse for everything.

Yeah, I'm afraid to have another baby because I'm afraid of the anxiety I'll experience being pregnant again. Even though the doctor said it's safe, I'm really scared of having another preemie baby. Plus, a third baby would just add another child to be anxious about all the time!

I just don't want to deal with the stress of it all. That promotion would cause my anxiety to go through the roof.

Yeah, I don't think I'm going to do that speaking gig. I have no clue what I'd talk about and the whole thought of it makes me stressed and anxious!

Oh, yeah, I've thought about starting a business or a podcast, but I have no idea where to start. The thought of it all makes me too anxious!

My anxiety was the reason I'd avoid so much, and I'd blame it for just about anything if I could. In all reality, it comes back to the whole anxiety about having anxiety thing. But here's the realization I've come to. Anxiety doesn't get to boss me around.

We've gone over twelve feelings now, one for each chapter. We've addressed all those feelings and learned how to combat them, or we've at least learned the truth about them. Your anxiety can be persistent in your life—some days more than others, sure. It can cause you to feel all twelve of those feelings. It can straight up rob you of your joy and make your life downright miserable if you let it. But anxiety doesn't get to dictate your life. When you declare this to Satan's face, you can break free from all of the lies he's spewing at you.

You're a mama who struggles with anxiety, but it doesn't get to be the boss over your life.

You only report to God.

Forget Taking Back My Joy—I Just Want to Be Healed

I hope since you've reached this point of the book, I've made it clear that your anxiety does not mean you're a failure as a Christian in any way. I should've made that loud and clear by now. However, you may still be thinking, *Why hasn't God healed me yet? Or when will He?*

Prayer is a big thing in our Christian lives. It's where we get our strength, but it's also where we make our requests to God. Then there's the thought process that if you don't get what you want, well, that must mean you're being punished for some sin you've committed. Right? Let's talk about that for a moment.

If I were to ask, "Lord, I want to be a size six," I wouldn't wake up the next morning and magically be able to wear those high-rise mom jeans (seriously, I don't understand why they're called that because they don't fit over my years-later postpartum belly). Whenever you pray, God looks at your motives behind what you're asking for (James 4:3). My motive here would be to magically decrease my waistline without any cardio work while still being able to eat all the mint chocolate chip ice cream I want.

What's your motive in asking to be healed of your anxiety? For me, sleep would be nice. It would be lovely not to obsess about things too. Not saying our motives are wrong here, but maybe, just maybe, the reason God hasn't healed you yet is this: You've gotta put in some work, girlfriend. You have to join the gym and say no to the ice cream if you want those size six jeans to fit (forget a six, I'd love to be an eight again). And when it comes to your anxiety, you've got to do the work to retrain your thoughts, seek your joy, and fight against your anxiety.

You've maybe got to seek treatment and accept the help of professionals. You've got to face the fears and train your brain that there's no real threat. You've got to lean into your relationship with God and rely on His strength. It. Takes. Work. Look at it through the eyes of your kids again; if you gave them everything they wanted right away, they'd never learn anything on their own. They'd never have to work for anything or learn the meaning of perseverance.

The same goes for us and our relationship with our Father. He's given us the tools to put in the work—His Word, therapists, doctors, etc. Now we have to put in some effort.

Here's another verse I found to help clear things up for you: "This is the confidence we have in approaching God: that if we ask anything according to *his will*, he hears us. And if we know that he hears us—whatever we ask—we know that we have what we asked of him" (1 John 5:14–15, emphasis added). If you're wondering why He hasn't answered your prayers for healing, remember that He is God—you are not. It's got to be *His* will and *His* way.

I can't tell you how many times I've prayed, *Lord, please put my anxious heart to rest*. It's part of my nightly prayer. Every. Single. Night. He knows how many times I've prayed for this, and some days He answers. Even if it's momentary rest for my anxious heart, it's still an answered prayer. It may not be the answer I'm expecting but it's the answer He knows I need because, after all, He knows what's best for me. I believe there is a purpose to your anxiety and it's not something God intends to waste.

Let's look at the story of Job for a moment. Job was a man of whom God said, "There is no one on earth like him; he is blameless and upright, a man who fears God and shuns evil" (Job 1:8). In one of the few recorded encounters between God and Satan, Satan challenged God by saying that Job had a cushy life and if he were to have lost everything, Job would surely have cursed the Lord (v. 11). God's response to Satan: "Very well, then, everything he has is in your power, but on the man himself do not lay a finger" (v. 12).

Yeah, you read that right.

God gave Satan permission to take, destroy, and full-on curse Job. And Satan did his work. He destroyed Job's livestock and servants. All ten of Job's kids were killed at the same time. *Poof*. He left Job destitute in one fell swoop. Job's faith remained unshakable, and he did not blame God once. But Satan didn't stop there.

We see God and Satan meet again in chapter 2, with God telling Satan, "[Job] still maintains his integrity, though you incited me against him to ruin him without any reason" (v. 3). To which Satan responded, "Skin for skin! A man will give all he has for his own life. But now stretch out your hand and strike his flesh and bones, and he will surely curse you to your face" (v. 4–5). God's response? "Very well, then, he is in your hands; but you must spare his life"

(v. 6). Satan continued by afflicting Job with painful sores all over his body. Job eventually entered a depression, cursing the day he was born. Job was stricken with so much pain and suffering, he called out to God, "Why me?"

You're probably thinking, *Well, this is a horrible story, Courtney, and doesn't reflect the God I know. Why would God intentionally let Satan do anything horrible to one of His children?* I know, it's probably one of the most difficult books of the Bible I've ever read. Job was blameless and a faithful servant of God who turned away from evil, so it's not as if God was trying to punish him. Let's hit that point further home here: Job didn't suffer because he was being punished for sin or a lack of faith. Okay, you got that?

Although Job was blameless, all his pain and suffering had a purpose. Through it all, God reminded Job that only He is God and He's all-powerful and all-knowing. God's plans are always good, even if they don't seem like it in the middle of suffering. Job was humbled, and God blessed the last part of Job's life with more blessings than he previously had. Job went on to have more children, more fortunes and wealth, and he died an old man. (He went on to live another 140 years after all these events.)

Back in His day, Jesus was known for His healings and miracles. People literally chased Him down and wanted nothing more than to just touch His clothes to experience His healing power. Luke 13:10–13 tells the story of a woman who was bent over and crippled for eighteen years. She could not stand up straight. Jesus knew she had suffered for many years. He knew the pain she had endured, so He put His hands on her and said, "Woman, you are set free from your infirmity" (v. 12). *Boom*—He heals her! She could've been healed many years before if God had wished, but that wasn't her story. Her suffering had a reason, I'm sure, and her story was meant to interweave into the very pages of the Bible. God's work was shown through her in just a few verses.

I recently heard a story of Jesus's healing work on another. *Poof*, the disease was gone. After listening to the story, I had mixed feelings. Sure, I was happy for this person to be set free of their illness, but part of me felt . . . jealous? Angry, perhaps? It was one of those situations where I found myself asking *Why them, and why not me? Am I praying wrong? Did I do something wrong? Why not me too, God?* There were a lot of mixed emotions, so I had to pray about it.

> *Dear God, I'm grateful You healed this person. I'm grateful You healed my mother of her breast cancer. I'm grateful You heal me and my family from every cold, virus, and other boo-boos. Lord, I know You have the power to heal, and You're so good at it. I know there's some reason why it's not Your will for me to be 100 percent healed from my anxiety. So I will continue to be anxiously joyful because I know my anxiety keeps me closer to You and You use it all for Your good either way. Thank You, Lord, for Your comfort, Your strength, and Your peace. I pray in Jesus's name, amen.*

I know it's a heavy question to ask why Jesus won't heal me. I know it sometimes makes me question my faith and even puts doubt in my heart. And while I don't have a straight answer as to if or when you'll ever be healed this side of heaven, I know He can use your anxiety for good.

My purpose is to take my mental illness and help others. That's how God is going to turn this all for good. I may have seasons where my anxiety is not as bad and other seasons where it's at an all-time high. I may have to rely on medication or counseling for years to help me cope. But I pray I will be rewarded for my perseverance. I'll always pray He will give me peace. But more than anything, I pray He will use my anxiety for His glory. I pray He will use me to help other anxious mamas out there somewhere. He turns *everything* for good (Rom. 8:28).

So if you've gotten to the end of this book and you're like "Forget taking back my joy—I just want to be healed," I want you to remember that you may be waiting to be healed, but God will not waste any time in the waiting.

Think for a moment about how much waiting there is in the Bible. From the time Adam and Eve first sinned all the way until Jesus's birth (I couldn't tell you this one but we're talking thousands of years). From the time the Israelites were first enslaved in Egypt until Moses parted the Red Sea (430 years to be exact). From the time the Israelites wandered in the desert until God actually gave them the promised land (40 years). From the first time Isaiah prophesied about Jesus until the first pages of the New Testament when the angel told Mary she would give birth to the Son of God (approximately 700 years). From the time of Jesus's death on the cross and His resurrection until His return (oh wait, that's right, we're *still* waiting for Jesus's second coming).

There's been a lot of waiting.

And what does God do in the waiting? He makes everything beautiful in its time, and no one can fathom what He does from beginning to end (Eccles. 3:11). God does His best work in the waiting. He brings us closer to Him. God tells a story within the stories and brings it all back together from beginning to end. We just have to run the race with perseverance and faith, keeping our eyes on Jesus (Heb. 12:1–2). He is showing us how faithful He is throughout it all, and we have to trust that He'll make it all beautiful when it's time.

Here are a couple passages to back me up in all of this:

And since we are his children, we are his heirs. In fact, together with Christ we are heirs of God's glory. But if we are to share his glory, we must also share his suffering.

Yet what we suffer now is nothing compared to the glory he will reveal to us later. (Rom. 8:17–18 NLT)

All this is for your benefit, so that the grace that is reaching more and more people may cause thanksgiving to overflow to the glory of God.

Therefore we do not lose heart. Though outwardly we are wasting away, yet inwardly we are being renewed day by day. For our light and momentary troubles are achieving for us an eternal glory that far outweighs them all. So we fix our eyes not on what is seen, but on what is unseen, since what is seen is temporary, but what is unseen is eternal. (2 Cor. 4:15–18)

And the God of all grace, who called you to his eternal glory in Christ, after you have suffered a little while, will himself restore you and make you strong, firm and steadfast. (1 Pet. 5:10)

Christ suffered for us; we're going to suffer a little bit here too. And it's all for our benefit. Eternal joy and peace are in heaven. I don't know the date for when you or I get there, but that's where the hope of true healing rests.

I'm going to say that again: Healing is coming. Heaven is where we will all experience eternal peace. No more panic attacks. No more racing heart or mind. Just peace and Jesus—forever.

Okay, here's another thought I have for you. If you're only looking for healing, perhaps focusing on your joy is where you will find it. Proverbs 17:22 says, "A joyful heart is good medicine" (CSB). *Joy* is good medicine. The best medicine! When you focus on taking your joy back from your anxiety, that joyful medicine may very well heal you or bring you closer to coping with your anxiety.

Healing doesn't come overnight. Healing can be miraculous, yes, but a lot of times, you have to take the steps (baby steps) to get control back from your anxiety. You have to choose to say, "No, anxiety, you're wrong. Those lies you're telling me are wrong. Jesus is the truth. So back off."

My counselor once asked me if healing was the end goal for me. Years ago, I would've said yes, most definitely. However, as I've gone through this journey of taking my joy back, my response to her was, "No, not really." I choked back some tears of joy. "Without my anxiety, I don't know if I'd have the same relationship with God that I do now. So I'm just gonna be anxiously joyful about it all."

Anxiously joyful.

That's just my perspective on all this. And God may heal you here on earth; I'm not saying it's not possible. But in the words of Shadrach, Meshach, and Abednego as they were about to be thrown into a fiery furnace because they worshiped God, "Even if he does not" (Dan. 3:18).

Even if He does not heal you, He is still your strength.

Even if He does not heal you, He is still your comfort.

Even if He does not heal you, He is still faithful to you and will see you through it all.

Even if He does not heal you, He is still the source of your joy.

Hey Anxiety, It's My Joy and I'm Taking It Back

I have been wracking my brain, trying to figure out how to wrap this all up. How do you finish a book and put a nice little bow on it, you know? I kept praying that God would point me to a story in my life—a defining moment when I took my joy back from my anxiety. I even asked, *Lord, has it even happened yet? Is this a part of my story that You're still writing?*

And then it hit me.

Every moment came flooding back to me. He was answering my prayer with all of it. The moment I decided to seek God in my life again, and begin writing about Him and my mental illness. Sharing my story with others even though I was afraid of the judgment. The moment when I called my doctor and asked to get back on my medication. The first time I took both my kids to Target after bouncing back from COVID-19. The first time I got to have a normal life experience for a stay-at-home mom with my kids after being in isolation for so long. The first time I met with my counselor and felt like I had found someone who truly understood me and had compassion for me. The first time I walked into church after quarantining my family for so long. Seeing another face smile back at me without a mask on, listening to the worship music live and in person versus in my pajamas in my living room. (Yes, I'm going there.) The first time I drank from a Starbucks cup without the assistance of sanitizer.

So many beautiful moments. Hitting "submit" on my book proposal and sending it out to fifteen agents and praying it found the right agent's hands. Boy, am I so grateful it did! Joining a small group even though I was terrified of people and socially awkward. (Some things never change, though.) Volunteering to coach and lead women at my church. Even though I felt completely unqualified for it and anxious about doing so, I still took the step because I knew God would equip me and lead me. The moment when I decided that my having another baby is up to God and His perfect plan. Making the decision that the fear of my anxiety heightening again and that I may revert was not a reason not to have baby number three.

There was not one defining moment when I took my joy back from my anxiety. It's been every moment I have *chosen* to take my joy back instead of listening to my anxiety.

It's looking your anxiety straight in the face and saying, "Uh-uh, anxiety, you're not taking my joy in this moment, this day, this week."

It's a continual process of seeking my joy over my anxiety.

It's continually choosing His peace over my fear.

It's continually seeking His presence and strength when anxiety starts to take over.

Anxiety does not get to win.

I'm going to be honest (again). During the whole process of writing this book, I've been on this journey with you, Mama. When I first pitched this idea to an agent, I was still crippled by my anxiety. I submitted it even though I knew I wasn't healed. I've been right here with you—typing the words out—as I've been journeying my way back to joy. And here's what I can tell you now as I'm wrapping this all up.

It's been months since my last panic attack. It's been a long time since I was unable to function in the world. I'm involved in my church, and I'm making friends. I'm sending my son to school for the first time, and I'm terrified about not having my eyes on him. But I know God is watching over him. I still struggle to sleep sometimes, but what mother doesn't? I still occasionally (okay, more often than not) feel my chest get tight and snap at my kids when I feel my anxiety heightening. It's still there—anxiety. But it's quieter now. It's not as persistent and it sure isn't controlling my life.

I may never be healed. I said it at the very beginning in the introduction. However, my faith in God has never been stronger, I'll tell you that much. I'm filled with joy and constantly thanking Him for all of His blessings and His faithfulness. I'm soaking in every moment with my kiddos, and my mind is set on the mission before me—raising disciples. I'm doing what He's called me to do. I'm taking my anxiety and glorifying Him like crazy throughout it all.

Anxiety may always be there.

But when it's great within me, I'm looking to Him to comfort me . . .

And bring me joy.

Baby Steps

The Stuff to Think About

- Know that God alone is your strength, and He will comfort you in your times of anxiousness—that's how you take your joy back.
- Know your anxiety does not keep you from God but brings the two of you closer together—that's how you take your joy back.
- Acknowledge that even if you're never 100 percent healed, your anxiety can be used for a purpose and for good—that's how you take your joy back.

- Learn to cope with your anxiety rather than let your anxiety take the driver's seat—that's how you take your joy back.

The Stuff to Try Out

- Spend time with God and be in His presence. Spend time in God's Word and prayer—just be with Him. First Chronicles 16:27 reads, "Splendor and majesty are before him; strength and joy are in his dwelling place." Psalm 16:11 reads, "You make known to me the path of life; you will fill me with joy in your presence, with eternal pleasures at your right hand." Where you'll find God, you'll find joy (little hint, His presence is everywhere, not just in a church with a steeple). And yes, I know you're a mom and there's not a lot of quiet time in your house if you have littles at home. Even if you're listening to worship music while doing the dishes, you're still in His presence. Seek Him and you'll find your joy.
- Try focusing on gratitude and all the blessings in your life instead of your current suffering. Focus on the joy of it all to help minimize the anxiety over the unknowns and what-ifs.

The Truth about It

> For I am the LORD your God
> who takes hold of your right hand
> and says to you, Do not fear;
> I will help you. (Isa. 41:13)

> When anxiety was great within me,
> your consolation brought me joy. (Ps. 94:19)

Dear God,
I pray for the mama who has just finished this book (yay!).
I pray this mama is equipped with Your truth for all the lies
and for all the feelings she has regarding her anxiety. I pray

she knows she is not less loved by You because of her anxiety, and I pray she knows You will bring joy out of her struggles. You turn everything for good. You're just so good. I pray she has the strength to face her anxiety head-on, to no longer feel ashamed of it, and to no longer feel weak if she chooses to seek help from a professional. I want her to love every bit of herself including that finicky amygdala or those wacky imbalanced chemicals in her brain. I pray she goes forth and shares her struggles, points others to You through her story, and comforts others with the same comfort she receives from You. I pray she continuously seeks her joy over her anxiety every day. I pray by now she's ready to take her joy back and to no longer let her anxiety boss her around. I pray she steps out of the constraints of her crippling anxiety and into joy. I thank You, Lord, for Your peace and joy every day in motherhood and until the end of time. I pray in Jesus's name, amen.

Acknowledgments

To my Jesus: From the pit of depression to the crippling fear of anxiety, You've never left my side. From the panicked delivery room to the quiet moments of rocking a baby to sleep, You've been there through it all. The very fact that I'm writing these words—it's all owed to You. Writing about You brings me such joy, and it's an honor that I do not take lightly. Thank You for placing this book in my heart and thank You for the power of the Holy Spirit guiding me through what to write and nudging me to dig deep inside myself and spit this book out. I pray this book glorifies You and helps bring the mama with anxiety closer to You.

To my Billy, the man who loves me just like Jesus—with all my flaws and weird little quirks: You're my best friend, the love of my life, anxiety partner, and boy, do you get me. I remember the first time you read the introduction to this book, and you said, "I think you're going to do this. It sounds like an actual book!" I laughed at you and said, "Ha! Yeah, right!" Thank you for believing in me and being my first editor. (Although I didn't always take the criticism gracefully, of course; I'm stubborn.) Thank you for being my biggest fan and pushing me to see this dream come true. Thank you for holding me during the panic attacks and talking to my anxiety pretty much every day. Thank you for being the best daddy to our kids. Gosh, I'm sure grateful God brought you all the way to Montana to find me. I love you, honey.

To my children, William and Adelyn: Thank you for taking all the naps and watching all the Netflix while Mommy wrote and put this book together. In all seriousness, though—I thank God every day for picking me to be your mama. I pray you always remember how much He loves you and that He is watching over you always. You're never alone. You kids are my greatest worries in life, that's for sure, but you're also my greatest joys. You're my everything, and Mommy loves you so much. Don't ever forget that.

To my agent, Rachel: Thank you for seeing the potential in me and this message. The rejections from other agents ranged from "you're not a mental health professional" to "you don't have a big enough platform," but you kicked all those aside and said, "Yes, girl!" And I am forever grateful for your yes. Thank you for believing in me and cheering me along!

To my publishing team at Revell: Thank you for championing me and believing in this book from the start. When my agent told me which publishers she was going to pursue, I heard a little whisper in my mind say, "It's Revell." I knew you were the team I wanted to help make this book a reality. (Hopefully, I didn't make it too hard on you all as a first-time author, but I truly appreciate all of your support! God bless you!)

To my mom: Thank you for raising me and leading me to Jesus. I would not be the woman I am today without you. I love you more, Mommy!

To my sister, Caitlin: Not only do I get to thank you for being my amazing photographer and capturing some genuine headshots, but I also get the honor to call you my sister! I love you, and I'm so grateful for you.

To my best friend, Lindsey: Thank you for cheering me on from the very beginning of this writing endeavor. From equipping me with "writer gear" when I first started blogging to praying for me as I started submitting my book proposal, you are ah-mazing. Even though we are miles and miles apart, you are my sister and I love you!

To my new friend, Maggie: Thank you for taking the time to sit down and review some of my theology with me. I had some major doubts about my ability to interpret Scripture, but you lessened my anxiety and gave me the validation that maybe I do know what I'm doing! I am so grateful for you, my friend.

To the rest of my family and friends: Thank you for loving this wacky girl and all her anxiety. Thank you for loving me, cheering me on, and believing in me. Thank you for being my people. I know you'll all be the first ones to buy this book and read it with love, so I thank you for that as well.

To my readers: Thank you for following along on this journey. Not every meme looked pretty, and not every blog post was perfectly punctuated, but I'm so grateful that anyone reads my words. When I set out on this writing journey, my goal was to reach one mama with my words and have her be encouraged. I pray that she is you, and I pray this book did more than just encourage you; I pray that it gave you comfort for your anxiety.

To my counselor, Ashley: Thank you for helping me seek joy over my anxiety. Thank you for being there for this journey and helping me cope with this brain of mine. And thank you for your compassion and wisdom.

To my church family: Thank you for accepting anxiety for what it is, a flaw in my brain. I'm grateful to be a part of a church community that has never once told me to "pray it away" but that has met me with loving arms and support.

To my writer/blogger friends: Thank you for cheering me on, sharing my words, and teaching me how to always believe in myself and my dreams. Although we've never met in real life, I feel such privilege to call you sisters. I pray you chase the dreams God has placed in your heart and never stop sharing your words with the world.

Appendix

For When Mama's Anxiety Is Stealing Her Joy

For When You're Needing Comfort for Your Anxiety

The LORD is my shepherd, I lack nothing.
　　He makes me lie down in green pastures,
he leads me beside quiet waters,
　　he refreshes my soul.
He guides me along the right paths
　　for his name's sake.
Even though I walk
　　through the darkest valley,
I will fear no evil,
　　for you are with me;
your rod and your staff,
　　they comfort me. (Ps. 23:1–4)

The LORD is my strength and shield.
　　I trust him with all my heart.
He helps me, and my heart is filled with joy.
　　I burst out in songs of thanksgiving. (Ps. 28:7 NLT)

Cast your cares on the Lord
    and he will sustain you;
he will never let
    the righteous be shaken. (Ps. 55:22)

When anxiety was great within me,
    your consolation brought me joy. (Ps. 94:19)

Peace I leave with you; my peace I give you. I do not give to you as the world gives. Do not let your hearts be troubled and do not be afraid. (John 14:27)

Cast all your anxiety on him because he cares for you. (1 Pet. 5:7)

For When You're Worried about the Future

Trust in the Lord with all your heart
    and lean not on your own understanding;
in all your ways submit to him,
    and he will make your paths straight. (Prov. 3:5–6)

Many are the plans in the mind of a man,
    but it is the purpose of the Lord that will stand. (Prov. 19:21 ESV)

"For I know the plans I have for you," declares the Lord, "plans to prosper you and not to harm you, plans to give you hope and a future." (Jer. 29:11)

Therefore do not worry about tomorrow, for tomorrow will worry about itself. Each day has enough trouble of its own. (Matt. 6:34)

For When You're Filled with Fear

Have I not commanded you? Be strong and courageous. Do not be afraid; do not be discouraged, for the Lord your God will be with you wherever you go. (Josh. 1:9)

I sought the Lord, and he answered me;
>   he delivered me from all my fears. (Ps. 34:4)

When I am afraid, I put my trust in you. (Ps. 56:3)

So do not fear, for I am with you;
>   do not be dismayed, for I am your God.
I will strengthen you and help you;
>   I will uphold you with my righteous right hand. (Isa. 41:10)

For I am the Lord your God
>   who takes hold of your right hand
and says to you, Do not fear;
>   I will help you. (Isa. 41:13)

For When Your Anxiety Is Keeping You Up at Night

In peace I will lie down and sleep,
>   for you alone, Lord,
>   make me dwell in safety. (Ps. 4:8)

I will bless the Lord who counsels me—
even at night when my thoughts trouble me. (Ps. 16:7 CSB)

He will not let your foot slip—
>   he who watches over you will not slumber. (Ps. 121:3)

For When You're Obsessing

Who of you by worrying can add a single hour to your life? (Luke 12:25)

Do not be anxious about anything, but in every situation, by prayer and petition, with thanksgiving, present your requests to God. And the peace of God, which transcends all understanding, will guard your hearts and your minds in Christ Jesus. (Phil. 4:6–7)

Notes

Chapter 1 I'm a Mom—It's My Job to Worry

1. Carmen P. McLean, "Gender Differences in Anxiety Disorders: Prevalence, Course of Illness, Comorbidity and Burden of Illness," National Library of Medicine, *Journal of Psychiatric Research* 45, no. 8 (August 2011): 1027–35, https://www.ncbi.nlm.nih.gov/pmc/articles/PMC3135672/#__abstractid681120title.

2. "Anxiety Disorders," Office on Women's Health, last revision February 17, 2021, https://www.womenshealth.gov/mental-health/mental-health-conditions/anxiety-disorders#.

3. Erika Barba-Müller, Sinéad Craddock, Susanna Carmona, and Elseline Hoekzema, "Brain Plasticity in Pregnancy and the Postpartum Period: Links to Maternal Caregiving and Mental Health," National Library of Medicine, *Archives of Women's Mental Health* 22, no. 2 (2019): 289–99, https://www.ncbi.nlm.nih.gov/pmc/articles/PMC6440938/.

4. "Anxiety Disorders," National Institute of Mental Health, last reviewed April 2022, https://www.nimh.nih.gov/health/topics/anxiety-disorders.

5. "Generalized Anxiety Disorder: When Worry Gets Out of Control," National Institute of Mental Health, last revision 2022, https://www.nimh.nih.gov/health/publications/generalized-anxiety-disorder-gad.

6. Kimberly Holland, "Amygdala Hijack: When Emotion Takes Over," Healthline, last revision September 17, 2021, https://www.healthline.com/health/stress/amygdala-hijack.

7. Kristeen Cherney, "Effects of Anxiety on the Body," Healthline, last revision August 25, 2020, https://www.healthline.com/health/anxiety/effects-on-body#Cardiovascular-system.

Chapter 2 Mommy Sometimes Gets Scared Too

1. Katherine Weber, "Rick Warren: Why God Encourages Christians to 'Fear Not' 365 Times in the Bible," *The Christian Post*, April 30, 2016, https://www.christianpost.com/news/rick-warren-why-god-encourages-christians-to-fear-not-365-times-in-the-bible.html.

2. "Repetition," Literary Terms, June 1, 2015, https://literaryterms.net/repetition/.

Chapter 3 No, Really, My Anxiety Isn't in Control of Me—I Just Have to Control Everything

1. *Frozen*, directed by Chris Buck and Jennifer Lee (Burbank, CA: Walt Disney Animation Studios, 2013).

Chapter 4 I Must Not Be Praying Right

1. Courtney Devich, "The Last 6 Months Have Taken My Anxiety to a Whole New Debilitating Level," *Her View From Home*, September 12, 2020, https://herviewfrom home.com/anxiety-to-a-whole-new-level/.
2. *Merriam-Webster*, s.v. "sin (*n.*)," accessed April 3, 2022, https://www.merriam -webster.com/dictionary/sin.
3. *Strong's Greek Lexicon*, s.v. "pneuma," Bible Hub, accessed April 4, 2022, https://biblehub.com/greek/4151.htm.

Chapter 5 #EpicMomFail

1. Natalie Shaw, *Daniel Tiger's Neighborhood: I'm Feeling Mad* (New York: Simon Spotlight, 2016), 2.
2. "Deep Breathing and Relaxation," The University of Toledo Counseling Center, accessed April 8, 2022, https://www.utoledo.edu/studentaffairs/counseling/anxiety toolbox/breathingandrelaxation.html.

Chapter 6 The Fear of Attack—a Panic Attack, That Is

1. Debra Jaliman, MD, "What Is Hematidrosis?," WebMD, medically reviewed January 26, 2022, https://www.webmd.com/a-to-z-guides/hematidrosis-hematohidrosis.
2. Carly Vandergriendt, "What's the Difference Between a Panic Attack and an Anxiety Attack?," Healthline, last updated October 19, 2022, https://www.healthline .com/health/panic-attack-vs-anxiety-attack.
3. "Panic Disorder: When Fear Overwhelms," National Institute of Mental Health, last revision 2022, https://www.nimh.nih.gov/health/publications/panic-disorder -when-fear-overwhelms.
4. Sarah Bence, "What Is an Anxiety Attack?," Verywell Health, last revision February 5, 2021, accessed April 22, 2022, https://www.verywellhealth.com/anxiety-attack -5088600.
5. *Strong's Greek Lexicon*, s.v. "paráklētos," Bible Hub, accessed June 3, 2022, https://biblehub.com/greek/3875.htm.
6. "Panic Attacks and Panic Disorder," University of Michigan Health Michigan Medicine, last updated February 9, 2022, https://www.uofmhealth.org/health-library /hw53796.

Chapter 7 I've Got a Lot Going On—My Mind Is Racing

1. Kelli Bachara, "You Are Not Your Anxiety," October 8, 2019, in *The Unraveling Podcast*, mp3 audio, 16:02, https://podcasts.google.com/feed/aHR0cHM6 Ly9mZWVkcy5idXp6c3Byb3V0LmNvbS81NDgzOTUucnNz/episode/QnV6en Nwcm91dC0xODMwMDA0?ep=14&fbclid=IwAR26QsynJ167_ft4D6SSTakK9oHjl T5fzOEckmb6adRl9oixOuFbIx4tyI4.

2. Aaron Kandola, "What Are Intrusive Thoughts?," MedicalNewsToday, updated October 27, 2022, https://www.medicalnewstoday.com/articles/intrusive-thoughts.

3. *Strong's Hebrew Lexicon*, s.v. "lēḇ," Blue Letter Bible, accessed February 20, 2022, https://www.blueletterbible.org/lexicon/h3820/niv/wlc/0-1/.

4. Sheldon G. Sheps MD, "Anxiety: A Cause of High Blood Pressure?," Mayo Clinic, March 8, 2022, https://www.mayoclinic.org/diseases-conditions/high-blood-pres sure/expert-answers/anxiety/faq-20058549#:~:text=Anxiety%20doesn't%20cause %20long,temporary%20spikes%20in%20blood%20pressure.

5. Zawn Villines, "OCD and Anxiety: What to Know," MedicalNewsToday, September 6, 2022, https://www.medicalnewstoday.com/articles/ocd-and-anxiety.

Chapter 8 Sorry, Kids—Mommy's Too Tired Today

1. "Sleep and Caffeine," American Academy of Sleep Medicine, last updated January 29, 2018, https://sleepeducation.org/sleep-caffeine/.

Chapter 10 I'm Just Over Here All by Myself

1. Beth Salcedo, MD, "The Comorbidity of Anxiety and Depression," National Alliance on Mental Illness, January 18, 2018, https://www.nami.org/Blogs/NAMI -Blog/January-2018/The-Comorbidity-of-Anxiety-and-Depression.

2. "Depression," Anxiety & Depression Association of America, accessed April 16, 2022, https://adaa.org/understanding-anxiety/depression.

Chapter 11 I Don't Need Help—I Have Jesus

1. *Strong's Greek Lexicon*, s.v. "hudrópikos," Bible Hub, accessed May 30, 2022, https://biblehub.com/greek/5203.htm.

2. Michael Rydelnik and Michael Vanlaningham, ed., *The Moody Bible Commentary* (Chicago: Moody, 2014), 1793.

3. "Facts and Statistics," Anxiety & Depression Association of America, accessed March 13, 2022, https://adaa.org/understanding-anxiety/facts-statistics#:~:text=Did%20You %20Know%3F,of%20those%20suffering%20receive%20treatment.

4. Jenev Caddell, PsyD, "5 Differences Between Coaching and Psychotherapy," Verywell Mind, last updated September 17, 2020, https://www.verywellmind.com /should-i-work-with-a-psychotherapist-or-coach-2337587.

Chapter 12 You Have My Eyes, but I Don't Want You to Have My Anxiety

1. "Anxiety and Depression in Children: Get the Facts," Centers for Disease Control and Prevention, last updated April 13, 2022, https://www.cdc.gov/childrensmental health/features/anxiety-depression-children.html#:~:text=Anxiety%20and%20de pression%20affect%20many,1.9%20million)%20have%20diagnosed%20depression.

2. "Anxiety and Depression in Children," Centers for Disease Control and Prevention.

3. "Data and Statistics on Children's Mental Health," Centers for Disease Control and Prevention, last updated March 4, 2022, https://www.cdc.gov/childrensmental health/data.html.